HANGING
RUTH
BLAY

HANGING
RUTH
BLAY

An Eighteenth-Century New Hampshire Tragedy

CAROLYN MARVIN

THE
History
PRESS

Published by The History Press
Charleston, SC 29403
www.historypress.net

Cover image: The author would like to clarify that the cover image does not depict Ruth herself, as no image of the actual hanging exists. The design is part of a woodcut by F.T. Merrill of the hanging of Mary Hibbs, from *A Book of New England Legends and Folklore*, by Samuel Adams Drake, 1874. *Courtesy of the Portsmouth Athenaeum.*

First published 2010

ISBN 978.1.5402.2083.7

]Marvin, Carolyn.
Hanging Ruth Blay : an eighteenth-century New Hampshire tragedy / Carolyn Marvin.
p. cm.
Includes bibliographical references.
ISBN 978-1-59629-827-9
1. Blay, Ruth, 1737-1768. 2. Infanticide--New Hampshire--Case studies. 3. Trials (Infanticide)--New Hampshire--Case studies. 4. Unmarried mothers--New Hampshire--Social conditions--18th century--Case studies. 5. New Hampshire--History--Colonial period, ca. 1600-1775. I. Title.
HV6541.U62N463 2010
364.152'3092--dc22
2010017201

Notice: The information in this book is true and complete to the best of our knowledge. It is offered without guarantee on the part of the author or The History Press. The author and The History Press disclaim all liability in connection with the use of this book.

Dedicated to the memory of Ruth Blay; her mother, Lydia Chase Blay; and all women who suffered the injustice of a biased justice system.

CONTENTS

CONTENTS

PREFACE

The story of Ruth Blay first caught my attention while cataloguing one of the nineteenth-century accounts of her hanging and discovering that our holdings at the Portsmouth Athenaeum also included a photocopy of the published broadside *The Declaration and Confession of Ruth Blay*. Upon reading that poignant document, which says so much while leaving so much unanswered, I felt such outrage at her fate that I felt compelled to discover the details of her case. More importantly, I wanted to uncover the real flesh-and-blood woman who had suffered the ultimate punishment—to understand Ruth as a woman of her time and give her back her voice.

Over the past three years, I have revisited Ruth's eighteenth-century New Hampshire in books, places, primary source documents and yes, in my imagination, for while I have learned much, much remains open to speculation. Attempting to trace the life of an ordinary, unmarried eighteenth-century woman is a daunting task, even when she met with an extraordinary end.

New Hampshire today remains one of two New England states (the other being Connecticut) that still has the death penalty on the books. The pros and cons are being weighed even as I write this, and a life hangs in the balance. Infanticide, unwanted pregnancies, abortion—the "crimes of women"; all of these remain controversial issues. If, indeed, we are to learn from the past in order not to repeat its errors, we must view history as a continuum rather than a group of events assigned to a particular span of time. Errors as well as glories tend to repeat themselves, and while history is often defined by events, it is lived by individuals—individuals like Ruth Blay.

Portions of this book were previously published in the spring 2009 issue of *Historical New Hampshire* as the article "The Hanging of Ruth Blay, December 30, 1768: Separating Fact from Fiction."

Acknowledgements

The author would like to acknowledge the following people for their encouragement and support: D-B Garvin, editor of *Historical New Hampshire*, for her ongoing help in getting Ruth's story told; Patti Craig, Deb Child and Courtney MacClachlan, for their encouragement, for joining me on field trips and for reading and commenting on the work in progress; Thomas Hardiman, for enduring multiple versions of the book and offering wise commentary; Susan DeGaia, for reading the text and for her kind remarks; Dennis Robinson, for introducing me and my subject to the press and publisher; Andrew Leibs, for his friendship and support through crises of confidence; and friends and family, for their "yes you can" attitude.

Introduction

THE END

> *Redeem the misspent life that's past,*
> *Live each day as if it were thy last.*
> *Then of thy talents take great care,*
> *For the last day thyself prepare.*[1]
> *−1767*

S tanding on the high ground in the northwest corner of the old South Cemetery, I look across the small pond below to catch glimpses of the salt waters of Little Harbor. The weather is cold but clear, and there is no forgiving cover of snow to soften the edges of the granite gravestones and the stubbled brown earth. It is December in the twenty-first century, but it is not difficult for me to summon up a vision of the area as it would have looked that day some 240 years ago when a thirty-one-year-old woman named Ruth Blay was brought here to be hanged.

On Friday, December 30, 1768, Ruth arrived at this same spot and faced in the same direction as she approached the gallows erected for her execution. With no headstones and few trees, there would have been a clear view to the harbor and open sea. Mercifully, that December was also milder than most, and the six inches of snow that fell on December 22 melted and was followed by above-freezing temperatures and rain. Not yet a cemetery, the land owned by the South Church was used as pasture

The north side of the pond in South Cemetery, Portsmouth, New Hampshire, taken from "Gallows Hill." Minus the trees and headstones, this would have been Ruth's last wordly view. *Photograph by Anthony Leibs.*

The End

and a military training ground. Farmer Samuel Hall, whose land abutted the field, was angered as the crowds trampled his stone walls to get to the site. The scaffold had been erected at the highest point of the land, and Hall would later seek, but be denied, recompense for the destruction that had been done by the crowds as they clambered or rode over his walls to position themselves as close as possible.[2]

People from Portsmouth and the surrounding towns would have risen early to attend the hanging scheduled to occur between the hours of ten and twelve. Imagine the curiosity seekers gathering on the hill to witness the hanging, jostling one another to better their view. Men, women and even children were there. Executions were well-attended events—cautionary theatre to warn the young of the dire consequences of flaunting the laws of God and king and entertainment of a macabre sort for others. And so they came, thousands of them according to reports, to witness the hanging of Ruth Blay.

Ruth spent her last dark evening at the prison that had been her home for more than five months, preparing a written statement witnessed by three persons. It is impossible not to feel saddened at the thought of her sheer exhaustion and despair, particularly on the eve of her execution. Then, with the first light on the morning of her last day, terror must have flooded her being. We have only hints at what she wore or how she behaved. While dressing well—as "brides of Christ," not uncommon for women who were publicly executed—whether Ruth dressed in silk, as mid-nineteenth-century retellings declare, cannot be verified.[3]

A horse-drawn cart carried her to the place of execution. Possibly it also carried the wooden casket in which she would be buried, as this was common practice. Its prisoner aboard, with hands tied, the cart left the prison, clattered along the Middle Road to Cow Lane, now Richards Avenue, and made its way to the field's entrance on South Street. A much later account states that her terrified "shrieks" could be heard throughout the city.[4] The cart was brought to a halt under the newly erected gallows. Ruth's supporters, hoping for a last-minute reprieve—a pardon even—must have looked anxiously in the direction of Governor Wentworth's home on Pleasant Street. Three reprieves had been granted previously, each one raising the hope of the condemned woman. But none came today.

Sheriff Packer, charged with the task at hand, was undoubtedly made nervous by the swelling crowd, a "vast concourse of people" according to

The End

news accounts,[5] many of whom may have been sympathetic to Ruth's cause. Among these would be persons discontented with the royal rule and harsh sentences meted out by British-appointed judges, those sympathetic to the growing Patriot cause and working-class or poor citizens who then, as now, could relate to the disparity of justice between the wealthy and the poor. They had been kept informed of Ruth's status since the beginning of the trial through newspaper accounts, in which she is referred to as "the unfortunate" or "the unhappy" Ruth Blay.[6] Whether any members of her family were present is unknown. It is not likely, as her mother and sisters lived a good distance away, and the pain they had already endured throughout the trial, along with the hope raised with each reprieve, would have made this final act unbearable.

The noose was placed around her neck; her hands and possibly her feet were bound. When hanging a woman, the skirt and petticoat were often tightly bound around her ankles to avoid a "lewd exposure" during the death dance (the jerky pre-death movements of the hanging body).[7] She would have been given time for a final prayer from the accompanying minister and any last words she may have wished to speak. It was reported in one newspaper that up to the end she was "in great Distress" before she was turned off, "begging for a few more Moments longer to live."[8]

The order was given to draw away the cart. Unless Ruth was fortunate enough to have had her neck broken by the fall, the sudden forward movement of the cart would have left her to drop and die of slow strangulation. The so-called long drop, which calculated body height to length of rope necessary to break the neck, had not yet been designed. In a few minutes it was over.

Sobered now by the completed act, the crowd would wait until she was pronounced dead before dispersing. At some executions, scavengers rushed to the lowered body to seize whatever might have been of value. It is doubtful that this occurred in Ruth's case. The amount of publicity about and opposition to Ruth's execution probably would have prevented this final desecration. After the crowds departed, Ruth's body was buried at the bottom of "Gallows Hill." She lies there today, undisturbed and unmarked but not forgotten.

What had she done, what great crime had she committed, that led her to these gallows? Simply stated, she had concealed the birth of her bastard child, who she claimed was stillborn—in so doing she had violated the existing law and placed her fate in the hands of the harsh provincial judicial system whose laws were written, defined and applied by men.

Ruth was a sempstress (seamstress) and a teacher, her mother Lydia, a tailor. The only tangible thing of hers remaining is a tattered piece of an indigo blue quilted petticoat. It seems fitting then, to stitch together the chapters of her story with sampler verses popular during her lifetime.

Chapter 1
THE BEGINNING

I live in a cottage & yonder it stands
And while I can work with these two honest hands
I'm as happy as those that have houses and lands.[9]
–1737

Eighteenth-century provincial New Hampshire was a sprawling frontier wilderness run by British governors and magistrates. It was founded as a business venture rather than a haven for religious dissenters, and the population was originally clustered in the coastal centers of Portsmouth, Dover Point and Gosport at the Isles of Shoals. Captain John Smith's early explorations in the 1620s produced maps that clearly showed the Isles of Shoals and Portsmouth, and by 1623 a fishing community existed at the Shoals.

Unlike the Plymouth and Massachusetts Bay Colonies, where land was granted to a corporation, the area comprising Maine and New Hampshire was granted to individuals. In 1622, the British Council for New England granted the land between the Kennebec River in Maine and the Merrimac and sixty miles inland from their headwaters to Captain John Mason and Sir Ferdinando Gorges. They, in turn, "sub-granted" parts of this vast territory to others. Another man, David Thomson, had also secured a smaller grant of six thousand acres and, in 1623, sailed from Plymouth, England, with the backing

Detail from a 1761 map of New Hampshire as surveyed by Samuel Langdon, showing the towns in which Ruth lived, worked and died. *Courtesy of the Portsmouth Athenaeum.*

PISCATAQUA HARBOUR

Isles of
Shoals

Great Boars Head

Hampton R. & Marshes

A Bar of Sand

Plumb
Island

Squam Harbour

Pidgeon Hill

Rocks called the
Salvages
Thatchers I.

Cape Ann
Cape Ann Harbour

Glocefter

hester

of three Plymouth merchants to find a suitable site for settlement. Thomson and others sailed on the ship *Jonathan* and founded the first settlement in New Hampshire at Odiorne's Point, at the mouth of the Piscataqua River.

Following the Piscataqua and its branches, the Cocheco and Lamprey, settlers moved inland from the southeastern coast to found the towns of Dover, Durham, Exeter and others. Along the border with the Massachusetts Bay Colony, other settlers followed the Merrimac River inland, and New Hampshire's population grew with a continuous migration of Massachusetts families seeking land, religious freedom or both.

A good example of the latter was the arrival in 1638 of John Wheelwright's group of Puritan dissenters, the Antinomians, who founded the town of Exeter. John, a minister in Quincy and the brother-in-law of Anne Hutchinson, took issue with the Puritan leadership's stand on his sister-in-law, was banished from Boston and then moved to Exeter.

Governing an area of many individual land grants proved difficult, and New Hampshire came under the governing body of the Massachusetts Bay Colony until 1680. From that date on, it had its own assembly and an appointed royal governor and/or lieutenant governor. By 1730, the provincial seat in Portsmouth was becoming wealthy from active trading in lumber, masts and fish. Those exports bought imports to sell, and the small coastal town grew and became home to many successful merchants, including members of the Wentworth family. The court system, too, was centralized in Portsmouth. New Hampshire was ready to be declared a political entity in its own right. When the boundary dispute between New Hampshire and Massachusetts was finally settled in 1741, Benning Wentworth was appointed the first royal governor of the new province of New Hampshire. Benning and his nephew, John Wentworth, who succeeded his uncle, remained in power until the outbreak of the American Revolution.

Meanwhile, north and west of Portsmouth, the bitter French and Indian Wars had introduced the colonists, albeit at a terrible cost, to the central and northern areas of New Hampshire and Vermont as they cut roads through to the Canadian border in pursuit of the enemy. The Peace of Paris in 1763 finally brought a close to the last of the French and Indian Wars. In another twelve years, alliances would alter, and the French would side with America in the revolt against British rule. Between the earlier wars, as each ensuing peace lessened the danger of Indian attacks, many colonists revisited, laid claim to and settled in these areas.

An Eighteenth-Century New Hampshire Tragedy

New generations of long-standing families who had settled in the parent towns along the coast and mouth of the Merrimac River acquired new property in the hills just a few miles inland, and family members ventured forth to establish these new townships, build meetinghouses in which to worship and raise new families to farm the land and create new communities. The land was hilly with rocky soil, the weather unpredictable and life a constant struggle lived under strict religious tenets as unforgiving as the land. Hard winters and summer droughts added to the homesteaders' trials. In Joshua Coffin's *History of Newbury, Newburyport, and West Newbury*—towns a short distance away from where Ruth grew up in the second parish of Amesbury (now Merrimac)—earthquakes and aftershocks are reported almost every year from the great one of 1727 through 1755 and thereafter.[10]

Order and status were established as leaders in each community emerged, were elected to responsible posts and fulfilled their elected or appointed duties. Families also brought with them the status of their birth families. As with all frontiers, migration north of the coastal communities brought hardworking persons of great esteem, as well as its share of those who were marginalized by reputation, bad luck, poverty or temperament. Despite the best efforts of church, town and Crown, there had always been those who could not or would not conform to accepted social mores or legal constraints.

The high mobility of our New Hampshire forefathers and foremothers often makes tracking these families a genealogical nightmare. Women like Ruth Blay, who didn't marry, had no brothers and whose sisters became absorbed into the families of their spouses, become even more difficult to track. Their surname effectively disappears.

Ruth began life in one of the Massachusetts border towns and later moved inland to live and work in today's New Hampshire towns including South Hampton, Danville and Sandown.

Fortunately, Ruth had grandparents who were among the earliest and most respected settlers of Newbury, Amesbury and Salisbury. Ruth's grandfather was John Chase, a son of Aquila Chase, one of the original proprietors of Newbury. Ruth's great-grandfather on her mother's side was Philip Watson-Challis, another well-respected early settler in Salisbury and Amesbury. Her great-grandmother, Mary Challis, an apparently educated and independent woman for her time, administered Philip's estate upon his death, and her name appears on a number of land transactions in her role as both family

Example of an eighteenth-century child's shoe, made by Samuel Lane of Stratham, New Hampshire. Ruth's father, a cordwainer, would have produced similar shoes and other leather items. *Courtesy of the New Hampshire Historical Society.*

matron and executrix. It was Phillip and Mary Watson-Challis's daughter, Lydia Challis, who would become Ruth's grandmother. Lydia Challis and John Chase were married in 1687 in what must have seemed a most auspicious marriage, merging two of the most prominent family names in the area. In time, they became the parents of nine children whose births are recorded in the Newbury church records.[11]

One of these children was Ruth's mother, also named Lydia, who was born in 1700. Unlike her brothers and sisters, who married cousins or persons with surnames common to the area, Lydia seems to have chosen a relative "outsider" as her spouse, one William Blay of Haverhill, Massachusetts.[12] Certainly he plied a respectable enough trade as a cordwainer (shoemaker), but he would have been of a lower economic class than Lydia, whose parents, while not wealthy, had certainly accumulated land, position and some material wealth, which can be ascertained from her father John Chase's itemized will proved in 1739: "Item I give unto my daughter Lydia five shillings to be paid by my executor out of my estate after my Decease (the Reason why I give her no more is because she hath had her Portion already."[13]

We can surmise that Lydia probably received the greater part of her "Portion," whatever that may have been, at the time of her marriage to William in 1724, perhaps allowing them to establish their homestead in the eastern part of Haverhill known as Rocks Village. Seven children, all girls, were born to the couple, their births duly recorded in church records.[14]

The tragedy of losing children touched most eighteenth-century families, and the Blay family was no exception. Two children died in infancy during the 1735 "throat distemper" (diptheria) epidemic; a third died in 1747. Three of the girls would marry. The last born was Ruth, named for an infant sister whose death preceded her birth. A not uncommon practice, it has been the bane of many a genealogist since.

Lydia Blay was thirty-seven years old at the time of Ruth's birth on June 10, 1737, an older mother by any standard. Baby Ruth's siblings were Ann, six; Abigail, seven; Lydia, twelve; and eldest sister Mary, age thirteen. In England, George II had been in power for one decade and British-born American Patriot and pamphleteer Thomas Paine was born. In America, Jonathan Edwards published *A Faithful Narrative of the Surprising Works of God in the Conversion of Many Hundred Souls in Northampton*, a work inspired by the beginnings of what would become known as the "Great Awakening."

Chapter 2

TESTING THE FAITH

I Have a God in Heaven
Who Care For Me Doth Take
And If I to Him Constant Prove
He Will Not Me Forsake.[15]
−1737

In the middle of the eighteenth century, the faith and endurance of the Blays and others was greatly tested by renewed war against the French, culminating in the successful 1745 siege on Fort Louisburg in Cape Breton and two other major events: the outbreak of a serious contagious disease and the concurrent arrival and spread of religious fervor known as the "Great Awakening." One of these we can prove had a direct effect on the young Blay family; the other we shall have to deduce may well have influenced the parents, if not the children.

The outbreak of "throat distemper" (diphtheria) was purportedly traced to the Clough farm in Kingston, where Mr. Clough had slaughtered a diseased hog in May. It then spread like wildfire throughout the surrounding communities:

The first person who took the disease was a Mr. Clough, who, having examined the swelled throat of a dead hog, died suddenly with a swelling in his throat...in fourteen towns in New Hampshire, nine hundred and eighty-four died between June, 1735, and July, 1736.[16]

The highly contagious disease took a devastating toll on the towns of southern New Hampshire, causing the death of over 1,000 persons, mostly children. In Haverhill alone, 199 persons died. The *New England Weekly Journal* for March 28, 1738, reported:

> *Just Published, the Second Edition, with Some Alterations and Additions, An Account of the Number of Deaths in Haverhill, and also some comfortable Instances thereof among the CHILDREN, under the late Distemper in the Throat; With an Address to the Bereaved. By the Rev. Mr. John Brown, Minister of the Gospel there.*[17]

We can imagine that the Blay family, being among the bereaved, may have attended that sermon or at least read Reverend Brown's published remarks. Their homestead was located on the eastern boundary of Haverhill, closer to Amesbury. In 1730, William was among twelve men who successfully petitioned the Haverhill church to release them to the second church of Amesbury (now Merrimac) so they might be closer to their meetinghouse.[18] This was common enough in the eighteenth century, when pioneers may have established homesteads miles from the nearest meetinghouse and attending Sunday service, an all-day affair, was difficult and dangerous.

Regardless of whether the Blay family heard Reverend Brown's accounting of the toll the throat distemper took, he and Lydia had suffered its devastation firsthand. A list of families who each lost two children includes the name of William Blay.[19] The vital statistics of Newbury records their names: Ruth and Ealce. They died in 1735.

In May 1738 a pamphlet was published in Boston with verses concerning the throat distemper epidemic and the toll it took on the region:

> *To Newbury O go and see*
> *To Hampton and Kingston*
> *To York likewise and Kittery*
> *Behold what God hath done.*

An Eighteenth-Century New Hampshire Tragedy

The bow of God is bent abroad
Its arrows swiftly fly
Young men and maids and suckling babes
Are smitten down thereby.[20]

With such clear evidence of God's displeasure with the direction in which this New World seemed to be headed, can it be any wonder that a spiritual "epidemic" would follow?

Chapter 3
THE GREAT AWAKENING

Remember time will shortly come
When we a strict account must give
To God the righteous Judge of all
How we upon this earth do live.[21]
−1737

The second of the major events affecting the general populace, and undoubtedly the Blay family as well, was the Great Awakening, which occurred in the mid-eighteenth century. The influence of this movement was felt up and down the Atlantic coast but especially in those colonies where traditional Congregationalism was practiced. Although not the first American revival movement, the revival of 1740, commonly called the Great Awakening, had by far the most long-term consequences. Other revivals had occurred after the great earthquake of 1727 and again in 1735 during the Connecticut River Valley revival—recorded and participated in by Jonathan Edwards. These were responses to particularly troubling times and events and tapped into the communal anxiety already present in the population. In addition to the devastating throat distemper, numerous earthquakes, illness, frightening storms and extreme seasonal temperatures laid the groundwork for an even more widespread religious revival movement.

As if on cue, this commenced with the arrival of the English itinerant minister Reverend George Whitefield, who came to America in the fall of 1740 and began to electrify congregations with his passionate fundamentalist sermons. He attributed the many catastrophes that the colonists had endured of late to a falling away from the strict tenets of the Bible and implored the people to leave their evil, lazy ways, renew their covenants with God and be reborn to the straight and narrow path of their faith. Whitefield appealed to those who sensed or feared a breakdown in the institutions that defined and monitored mores: the church, the town and the family.

Preaching his way throughout England and the New World, "harvesting souls" through the ritual of conversion and rebirth, he restated the plain truths of the Bible and exhorted people to reassess their faith as measured against these. He first appeared in Newbury on September 10, 1740. Even the weather that year seemed to portend of impending doom. The summer and fall rains caused the Merrimack River to rise fifteen feet, floating off houses and washing away all the shipbuilding wood. This was followed by the most severe winter on record. Mother Nature capped the unusual year of weather extremes with a December earthquake.[22]

Reverend Whitefield traveled throughout the northern and middle colonies preaching from meetinghouse pulpits and to larger crowds gathered outside in fields. That he possessed enormous charisma is indisputable. Listen to Nathan Cole, who left his fieldwork as soon as he heard that Whitefield was nearby, gathered up his wife and horse and hurriedly traveled the twelve miles to the outdoor revival in Middletown, Connecticut:

> *The land and the banks over the river looked black with people and horses all along the 12 miles…When I see Mr. Whitefield come upon the Scaffold, he looked almost angelical—a young, slim, slender youth before some thousands of people, and with a bold, undaunted countenance. And my hearing how God was with him everywhere as he came along, it solemnized my mind, and put me in trembling fear before he began to preach, for he looked as if he was Cloathed with authority from the great God.*[23]

While Whitefield was eagerly joined by other so-called New Light ministers in spreading the message, some were not as easily swayed by his passion. Indeed, many were even disturbed by his charismatic personality and the excesses of swoonings, visions and outcries during the revivals.

George Whitefield preaching. *Courtesy of the Portsmouth Athenaeum, Special Collections.*

They were clearly threatened and fearful of the disruption to their own congregations by him and other New Light preachers, most importantly Gilbert Tennent and rabble-rouser James Davenport. The latter joined Whitefield and later went off on his own, declaring certain installed ministers "unconverted" followers of the letter but not the spirit; he was repeatedly apprehended and even kicked out of one town after another for his inflammatory sermons against the Congregationalist clergy. He was censured by the ecclesiastical council and, after a few more years of frenzied sermons and actions, settled again in his parish, where he wrote his *Confession and Retractions* acknowledging his excesses.[24]

Clear proof of how threatened local ministers were comes in a letter written by Reverend Plant, minister of Queen Anne's Chapel in Newbury, to a Dr. Bearcroft: "I do not know but before these six months to come, most of my hearers will leave me for all the country near me is taken with this new scheme (as they call it) [Methodism]. Within one month fifty-three have been taken into communion in one dissenting meeting house."[25] This is followed by a reference to an ongoing dispute in the *Boston Evening Post* regarding New Light ministers coming into town and attempting to "take over" Mr. Lowell and Mr. Coffin's Newbury meetinghouses.[26]

However, in both Portsmouth and Newburyport, Whitefield was welcomed. Reverend William Shurtleff twice invited him to his South Church parish and recorded his impressions in a letter to Harvard classmates Sewall and Prince, stating, "I have frequent opportunities of being with him and there always appears in him such a concern for the advancement of the Redeemer's Kingdom and the souls."[27] In Newburyport, it was Whitefield who encouraged Jonathan Parsons, a zealous New Light, to establish a new parish among the separatists. This he did, founding the First Presbyterian Church in 1746.[28]

The divisions between educated, more "rational" and traditional members of the clergy and these New Light itinerant ministers stirred controversy throughout the church and extended to the hallowed halls of Yale and Harvard. At Yale, a third-year student was caught speaking against one of his tutors, whose delivery of a prayer had been "lukewarm" at best.[29] Although the remark was made privately among friends, the student, David Brainerd, was betrayed by someone and expelled from Yale; he devoted the remainder of his short life to missionary work among the Indians. After Brainerd's death in 1749 at the young age of twenty-nine, Jonathan Edwards published Brainerd's diary, and Brainerd became a folk hero among evangelicals.[30] Jonathan Edwards wrote in defense of the revivalists but cautioned against their excesses. While the Great Awakening divided the New England clergy, it contributed to thousands of conversions and the diversification of denominations throughout New England.

In simplest terms, the theological dispute was over the path to salvation: is one "saved" by performing regular Christian duties under ministerial guidance, or can one, indeed *must* one, be "elected" by rebirth through conversion. Many New Lights left their churches to join the Baptists, thus cementing the establishment of that sect in New England.[31] There was a renewed interest in studying for the ministry, and it seemed that on the whole, the revival had shaken the status quo and increased both church attendance and piety among the general populace.

Whitefield periodically returned to America to shepherd his many followers and met his death in Newburyport, Massachusetts, in 1770. After preaching three days in Portsmouth, Whitefield preached his last "field" sermon in nearby Exeter and then rode to Newburyport to stay with Presbyterian minister Jonathan Parsons. After enduring a severe attack of his chronic asthma, George Whitefield died in Parson's home in the early morning of September 30, 1770. He was just a few months short of his fifty-sixth birthday.

Word of his death spread quickly. Portsmouth's Dr. Haven brought an offer from Mr. Sherburne to pay for him to be buried in Portsmouth; Boston, too, offered to bring his body there for internment.[32] Whitefield, however, had requested that his body be buried beneath the Reverend Parson's pulpit should he die in Newburyport, and his wish was granted. More than six thousand mourners flooded Newburyport for Whitefield's internment on October 2. The bells tolled at one, two and three o'clock for the solemn occasion, and the ships in the harbor sounded horns. His remains were entombed beneath the pulpit, a cenotaph was erected in his memory in 1829 and today a lighted crypt holds a plaster cast of his Bible, with a plaster cast of a skull poised atop.[33]

Word of his death spread quickly in America and abroad, and mourners gathered to hear the many sermons preached on the occasion of his death. A young African American poet in Boston, Phillis Wheatley, even honored him with a poem (*On the Death of the Rev. Mr. George Whitefield, 1770*), a portion of which reads:

Hail, happy saint, on thine immortal throne,
Possest of glory, life and bliss unknown;
We hear no more the music of thy tongue,…

…we Americans revere
Thy name, and mingle in thy grief sincere;
New England deeply feels, the Orphans mourn,
Their more than father will no more return…

While the tomb safe retains its sacred trust,
Till life divine reanimates his dust.[34]

The cenotaph erected in 1839 in memory of George Whitefield inside the First Presbyterian Church in Newburyport, Massachusetts. *Photograph by author.*

An Eighteenth-Century New Hampshire Tragedy

The crypt under the pulpit in the basement of the First Presbyterian Church, showing the plaster casts of a skull and Bible, as well as a wall plaque memorializing the great itinerant preacher. *Photograph by author.*

The significance of the Great Awakening and its relevance to all the areas touching the settlers' lives is best summed up by Douglas Sloan:

> *The religious revival that swept the American colonies in the 1740's was so widespread, so unsettling, that it has been known ever since as the Great Awakening. As observers at the time noted, it was a "great and general awakening," leaving no social class, no section of the country, no church body untouched...although the issues of the Awakening were primarily religious...they were intertwined with virtually all of the important social, political and intellectual questions of mid-eighteenth century America.[35]*

The Great Awakening contributed to the "democratization" of religion and cemented the importance of religious liberty, which was easily translated to political liberty as the century wore on. Additionally, it contributed greatly

Hogarth print entitled *Credulity, Superstition and Fanatacism*, 1762. *Courtesy of the Portsmouth Athenaeum.*

to the conversion of the native populations and the founding of colleges like Dartmouth, Princeton and Brown.

Echoes of the Great Awakening continued to reverberate in a series of "after-shocks" well into the 1760s. In 1755, following the drought suffered the previous year, Hannah Sargent acknowledged her own spiritual drought and was converted. Rachel Low, shortly after the great earthquake of 1755, in fear of death and damnation confessed her sins and sought the ritual of conversion. She stated that the experience was "like a dart cast into my soul."[36] Samuel Buell and others along the New England coast from Ipswich to Rhode Island, took up the cause in the "Seacoast Revival of 1762–1765," just three years prior to Ruth Blay's hanging, thus contributing to a climate of renewed spiritual concern.[37]

It's impossible to know whether the Blay family ever heard the great revivalist Whitefield. Through the vital records kept by the Blay family parish, we know that they attended church and had all their children baptized. We know also that the Haverill minister was a New Light, gave a sermon following the diphtheria epidemic and had invited Whitefield to speak there. It is therefore almost inconceivable that they were not influenced by this revival, even if they had no direct contact with Whitefield. There would have been discussion and empathy among those who had lost their children during the epidemic, and questioning their faith and spiritual state would have been a natural response to this tragedy.

Revivals by their very nature are group experiences—the fervor is "catching," and one person in a family having experienced conversion, or groups of revivalists meeting in one another's homes, would be eager to spread the word of their rebirth and enlightenment to others. The pros and cons of the controversy were the subject of prolific published and unpublished sermons, letters to newspapers and general conversation. Indeed, it is difficult to see how the Blays could *not* have been affected by it. Whitefield was as well known and admired in his time as twentieth-century revivalists such as Billy Graham are in theirs.

Chapter 4

HOME AND FAMILY

Next unto God dear parents I address
My self to you in humble thankfulness
For all your care and charge on me bestowed
The means of learning unto me allow'd [38]
−1747

R uth would have been between three and five years old during the
period of the Great Awakening, which might seem too young for
her to have been personally affected by it. Yet, as we shall see, it would be
another impressionable five-year-old who would be forever marked by her
own role in Ruth's tragedy.

Near the end of this initial revival period, in 1742, the Blays suffered yet
another blow when father William died. Fortunately, he died testate, and his
will of 1738 is recorded in the Essex County probate records. In it he leaves
to his "well beloved wife Lydia, (whom I likewise Constitute, Make and
Ordain my sole executrix of this my last will and testament) all and Singular
my Estate Both of Real and personal by her freely to be used and enjoyed
and to do with as she shall see cause to Dispose of the Estate," and he also
leaves to each of his surviving daughters—Mary, Ann, Lydia, Abigail and
Ruth—five shillings.[39] The will was proved in probate in September 1743.

William Blay's will gave Ruth five shillings. *From Essex County Probate Records, Phillips Library, Salem, Massachusetts.*

The significance of this event is not difficult to measure. As there were no sons, William entrusted the administration of his estate to his wife. While the homestead and nonitemized real and personal property is not described in detail, it was undoubtedly humble. After paying for a Christian burial (as requested in the will) and settling any outstanding debts, there was likely little left. For Lydia to hang on to this bequest while raising and settling five daughters into their own lives must have created great physical and emotional stress. Difficult enough with a husband by your side and ideally with sons as well, imagine what it must have been like to be left with five daughters. When she was widowed, Lydia was forty-three; Ruth, just six; Ann, twelve; Abigail, thirteen; Lydia, seventeen; and Mary, eighteen.

As Laurel Ulrich has so clearly expressed in her book *Good Wives*, the role of northern New England women in the colonial period was defined by the various roles they played: housewife, deputy husband, consort, mother, mistress, neighbor and Christian.[40] Clearly, Lydia exemplified this multiple-role definition of a good wife. Indeed, when William died, she went beyond "deputy husband" to become the surrogate head of the family and maintained that status for nine years, in addition to her duties as a homemaker, mother, neighbor, Christian, teacher and tailor. The two roles she no longer filled were ones that may have given her the most support and comfort: consort and mistress.

To be a widow, a "relict" with unmarried daughters in the 1700s, usually meant poverty and hardship, and so seems to have been the case for Lydia. Winter was coming on in the second parish, and Lydia needed to find ways to make ends meet. In later records, she is referred to as a "tailor," so perhaps the family was able to stave off poverty by this means. Other women of the time brought in a few extra shillings by selling butter and other farm goods, and Lydia may well have done the same. From the writings of other women, we can begin to understand the enormity of the task of running a crowded homestead. Vivid descriptions of the obligations that rural housewifery entailed are found in women's journals of the period.

Women's work on the average eighteenth-century homestead was determined by the day, week and season. Certain chores must be done daily: meals to prepare, the cow to milk, eggs to gather and a garden to tend. Weekly chores might include washing clothes, scrubbing the floors or sweeping them with sand and churning butter. Seasonally, a woman might plant the garden; gather and preserve crops, most often root crops that stored well through the winter; dry herbs, apples and other fruit; render lard; salt meat, either of their own or purchased; and make candles and perhaps cider. There never seemed to be enough time. And always, quite literally, keeping the home fires burning for cooking and heating. As Molly Cooper of Long Island complained in her diary in 1768, "It has beene a tiresome day to me. It is now bed time and I have not had won minuts rest today."[41]

Complaints of this type echoed throughout the eighteenth century women's world, from Martha Ballard in 1804 and Molly Cooper in 1771, respectively:

> *I have had to go thro' the wet to feed my hoggs, milk my cow, and pique my wood from the old loggs in the garden; and have sorted part of my apples; and sheld some corn; part washt my room, etc., etc.*[42]

> *The hail cesses this morning and floods of rain pores down with frightful gusts of wind which blew away parte of the kitchen. We have hardly a dry place in the house. I suffered much this day with the wet and cold, and am up all night.*[43]

Of course, then as now, some women took more pride in their skills and standards for good housewifery. Molly Cooper seemed to drive herself to conquer the dirt present everywhere and frequently grumbles about her fatigue. Other rural women, perhaps, were more accepting of the conditions in which they lived and were able to better tolerate them—or at least assign them a lower priority. In this type of chore at least, Lydia would have had some help from her daughters.

Lydia must have been an incredibly strong woman, physically and mentally, to have endured the sorrow that life had already handed her and to persevere in the face of the loss of William's companionship, his income and his work on the homestead. By the next summer, plans for the older girls had to be made. Their help around the home would have been welcome, and we can surmise that the girls were taught the usual domestic chores and social graces of housewifery. Given that Lydia had come from a literate family herself and that William signed his will with a fine hand, not a mark, we can speculate that they had also been taught the rudiments of reading and writing. It was a double-edged sword: the fewer the mouths to feed, the easier it would be for the widow to hold on to the homestead financially, but the more difficult it became in terms of the division of hard labor.

In July 1744, we find the first evidence of a Blay's presence in nearby South Hampton, New Hampshire. Records of "warnings out" found in the New Hampshire State Archives show that Richard Collins, constable for the town, sent notice to Ruth's sister, Ann Blay, that she, together with another "child," Ezra Howard, must leave town within fourteen days.[44] At the time, they were living with Moses Richardson, possibly being boarded as laborers. "Warning out" was a common legal practice in towns afraid of becoming financially responsible for persons outside the family nucleus. Only unpropertied people could be warned out of a community and returned to the town from which they came. While often the person being warned out was but one member of an entire family, in the case of Ann Blay it appears that she and Ezra were there without kin.

Warned-out individuals were rarely itinerants; they were nonresidents with no legal status living in households that had agreed to take them in for a variety of reasons—sometimes for the work they could perform on a homestead and often simply because they were friends or relatives. If relatives, and the family could prove that they could support them for a period of three months, they were allowed to remain and become inhabitants. Because women were the child bearers and because no town wished to bear

An Eighteenth-Century New Hampshire Tragedy

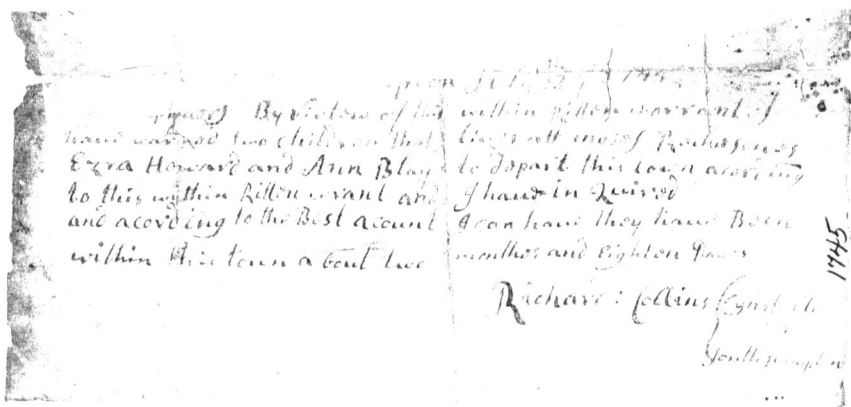

"Warning out" for Ann Blay and another child. State Archives. *Courtesy of the New Hampshire Division of Archives and Record Management.*

the additional costs of possibly supporting a bastard baby, they were often particularly targeted in the warnings. In a patriarchal society, women from matriarchal families who overstayed their welcome and were discovered or reported by a legal resident were quickly warned out and given notice to leave the town within the prescribed fourteen days.

The fact that Ann was warned out would lend support to the apparent poverty of the widow Blay. Ann was returned to her mother but would resume her connection to South Hampton seven years later when she married Samuel Carter of that town.[45] The marriage was duly recorded in the church records, but there the trail ends. No births or deaths of the Blay/Carters are recorded in that parish, and Ann was not called as a witness at her sister's trial.

Two years after William's death, Lydia was relieved of the support—but also the help—of two more of her daughters. In 1745, her eldest daughter, Mary, married Nathaniel Blaisdel of Chester, and sixteen-year-old Abigail wed Noah West.[46] We know that both Mary and Abigail remained in the area because they would be called as witnesses at their sister's trial.

The widow Blay's shrinking household was again diminished when her namesake daughter, Lydia, died in 1747 at the age of twenty-one, possibly also of the throat distemper that had again flared up. It was just four years later when Ann married Samuel Carter.[47] With only fourteen-year-old Ruth remaining, Lydia sold the homestead in 1752, having been able to hold on to it alone for an amazing nine years. In the account of the sale, she is described as a tailor.[48]

45

The fifty-two-year-old widow and her teenage daughter Ruth now had to decide where to reside and how to survive. Again, the lack of sons made this difficult for Lydia. Often, an older son would have land of his own and take in a widowed mother and any remaining single sisters. Where Lydia and Ruth lived during the fifteen years following the sale of their property is unknown. It seems most likely that they relocated to Chester and moved in with eldest daughter Mary and her husband Nathaniel.

While early homes of settlers of modest means were small, it was not uncommon for several generations to live together in crowded conditions. Of the married daughters, the Blaisdels were probably the best off economically. The Blaisdel family of Chester was well established and well respected. Nathaniel was a shopkeeper and had a house in addition to the store; his brother, Isaac, was a well-known clockmaker. Settled in 1720 by grantees from Haverill, Hampton, Newbury and Portsmouth, home lots of twenty acres each were laid out and paths cut through to Haverhill and Kingston. We know that William Blay traveled these roads doing business, as he is mentioned in a 1726 Chester will as one of several to be paid in settling the estate.[49] By 1758, Chester could boast nine schools (three of them dame schools) and, by 1767, a population of over 1,100.[50]

It seems most likely, then, that Ruth might have spent the intervening years in or near Chester, learning more needlework from her tailor mother, as well as improving her own literacy so that she could earn her keep by teaching. Teaching in dame schools was one of the few means that unmarried women had to support themselves, meager as the pay was.

Chapter 5

SEMPSTRESS AND TEACHER

A discreet person of good conversation.[51]
—definition of a teacher in 1719 New Hampshire law

Learning is an ornament
A portion never to be spent.
When land is gone and money spent,
Then learning proves most excellent.[52]
—1750

The years between 1752 and 1767 are the "missing years" in Ruth's life. As has been suggested, the family most probably moved to the Chester area to reside with her sister, Mary Blaisdel, and her family. We know from town records that Nathaniel was the most likely to have had room for them and that education was as valued there as it had been in Lydia's birth family, the Chases, several of whom became schoolmasters. There is mention in the Chester town records of payment being made to Nathaniel Blaisdel for boarding schoolmasters.[53] Lending further credence to their being in Chester is the fact that Ruth next appears as a paid teacher in the town records of both Hawke and Sandown, towns immediately bordering Chester.

The history of education in eighteenth-century New Hampshire is well defined by the laws of the period, although these laws mandated an ideal frequently impossible for towns to realize. In a 1761 publication, "Acts and Laws of His Majesty's Province of New Hampshire in New England," the law regarding education, which had been in effect since 1719, stated

> [t]*hat every town within this province, having the number of fifty householders, or upwards, shall be constantly provided of a school-master to teach children and youth to read and write. And where any town or towns have the number of one hundred families, or householders, there shall also be a grammar school set up and kept in every such town, and some discreet person of good conversation, well instructed in the tongues, shall be procured to be master thereof; every such school-master to be suitably encouraged and paid by the inhabitants.*[54]

Now the assembly understood that not all towns could comply with this law, but it is remarkable even in its intent. Education in New England was highly valued, if sometimes narrowly interpreted. If unable to comply, a town might petition for a waiver; failing that, they could be fined twenty pounds. The founding fathers and mothers were expected to value literacy at least to the extent that it made possible the reading of the Psalter and the Bible. Of all the colonies, New England in particular was quick to confirm the value of education by passing these early laws.

Regardless of what the law mandated, how children were taught was sometimes determined by gender, including even the basic precepts of Christianity. Oral instruction in religion could be provided at the hearth or spinning wheel, and the domestic and social skills of housewifery were deemed of the utmost importance to young women. Often, girls were taught in the summer months and boys and youth in the winter. Clearly this was in part determined by the usefulness of boys during the seasonal planting and harvesting and the importance of textile arts and food preservation and preparation during the winter.

What they were taught was also partially determined by gender. As stated, the domestic arts and the rudiments of reading and writing, especially of a religious nature, were deemed most important for girls. As women and mothers, the moral upbringing of children would be in their charge. Boys must learn reading and writing, as well as basic arithmetic, to serve them in future economic and legal transactions. The instructional books used by all children were those that philosopher John Locke referred to as the "Ordinary

Woodcut in frontispiece of *The New England Primer*, 1814. *Courtesy of the Portsmouth Athenaeum.*

Road" of instruction: the hornbook, primer, Psalter, New Testament and Bible.[55] Their souls were in as much jeopardy as their physical bodies, and adherence to Christian values and practice was their only hope for salvation. Reading the Bible provided a behavioral and moral template for Christian living. No separation of church and state here! These books literally put "the fear of God" in their little hearts and showed them the only path to the rewards of heaven.

Interestingly, another effect of the Great Awakening was seen in the increased number of books and pamphlets published and circulated after 1740. A journal of Whitefield's travels through the provinces became a period bestseller, along with reprints of Cotton Mather's works.[56] Smaller pamphlets and sermons throughout the second half of the century also enjoyed great popularity and were regularly printed in the newspapers of the time.

One concept developed in colonial New England to address the problem of providing education to all parts of these towns, where vast acres separated the homesteads, was that of the "moving school." It was a simple and effective idea. A teacher would board with a family and spend a few months teaching the children in one area of town and then move on to another. Thus every child's education was addressed on a rotating basis.

NEW ENGLAND PRIMER.   11

In Adam's fall
We sinned all.

Thy life to mend,
God's Book attend.

The Cat doth play,
And after slay.

A Dog will bite
A thief at night.

The Eagle's flight
Is out of sight.

The idle Fool
Is whipped at school.

A B C D E F

Learning to read, eighteenth-century style. *The New England Primer*, 1814. *Courtesy of the Portsmouth Athenaeum.*

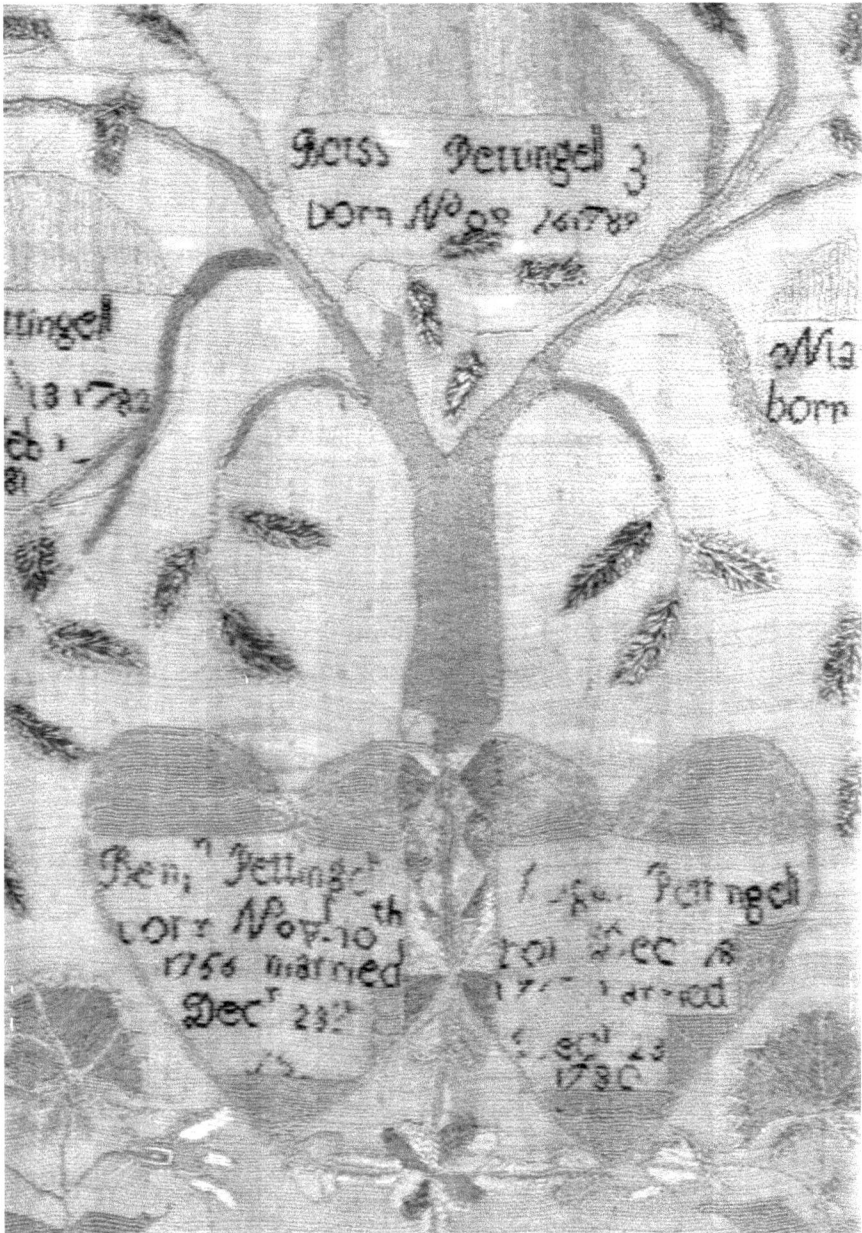

Pettingell family tree sampler from the late eighteenth century. The pattern is typical of those done in the area where Ruth lived and worked. *Courtesy of Robert Chase, York, Maine.*

"Dame" schools run by women, most of whom were spinsters or widows, were another common solution. Here the rudiments of reading and writing could be taught, as well as the fine art of needlework. Samplers are an excellent example of the way in which female literacy was taught and reinforced through the domestic skill of needlework. As previously mentioned, Chester was a town that took education very seriously, and by the time Ruth was of an age to teach, there were several regular schools and three dame schools.[57]

It is in this capacity in 1767 that Ruth Blay reappears in colonial records: first at Fitts Corner in the town of Sandown, just over its boundary with Chester, and later in neighboring Hawke (now Danville). In Sandown, Ruth was boarding with the families of Joseph Tilton and Robert Collins. For one term of teaching, she received twelve pounds, eighteen shillings and nine pence.[58]

In the following year, the records of the adjoining town of Hawke list her as a teacher there. It is possible that the towns shared her services. In March 1768, she received a final payment of three pounds for teaching in Hawke's northern district.[59]

Chapter 6

A Fall from Grace

But how my childhood runs to waste
My sins how great their sum
Lord give me pardon for the past
& strength for days to come.[60]
—1754

At some time during the fall of 1767, the now thirty-one-year-old teacher became pregnant. During the colonial period, pregnancy before marriage was not in and of itself shocking. It is estimated that during the pre-revolutionary era in many New England towns 30–40 percent of brides were pregnant.[61] For Ruth, however, it must have created an enormous amount of anxiety. Her position as a teacher, someone expected to be above reproach and to set an example for children, greatly complicated her dilemma. In addition, it appeared that marriage would not follow the revelation of her state of affairs.

Who the father might be and why she didn't marry or reveal his name may initially seem self-defeating. However, when you review the mores and laws of the time, you realize that the cards were stacked against her. Legally, Ruth would not be able to claim support from the man unless she uttered his name before a witness during the birthing. More significant was the likely possibility that this man was married—perhaps even a man of considerable

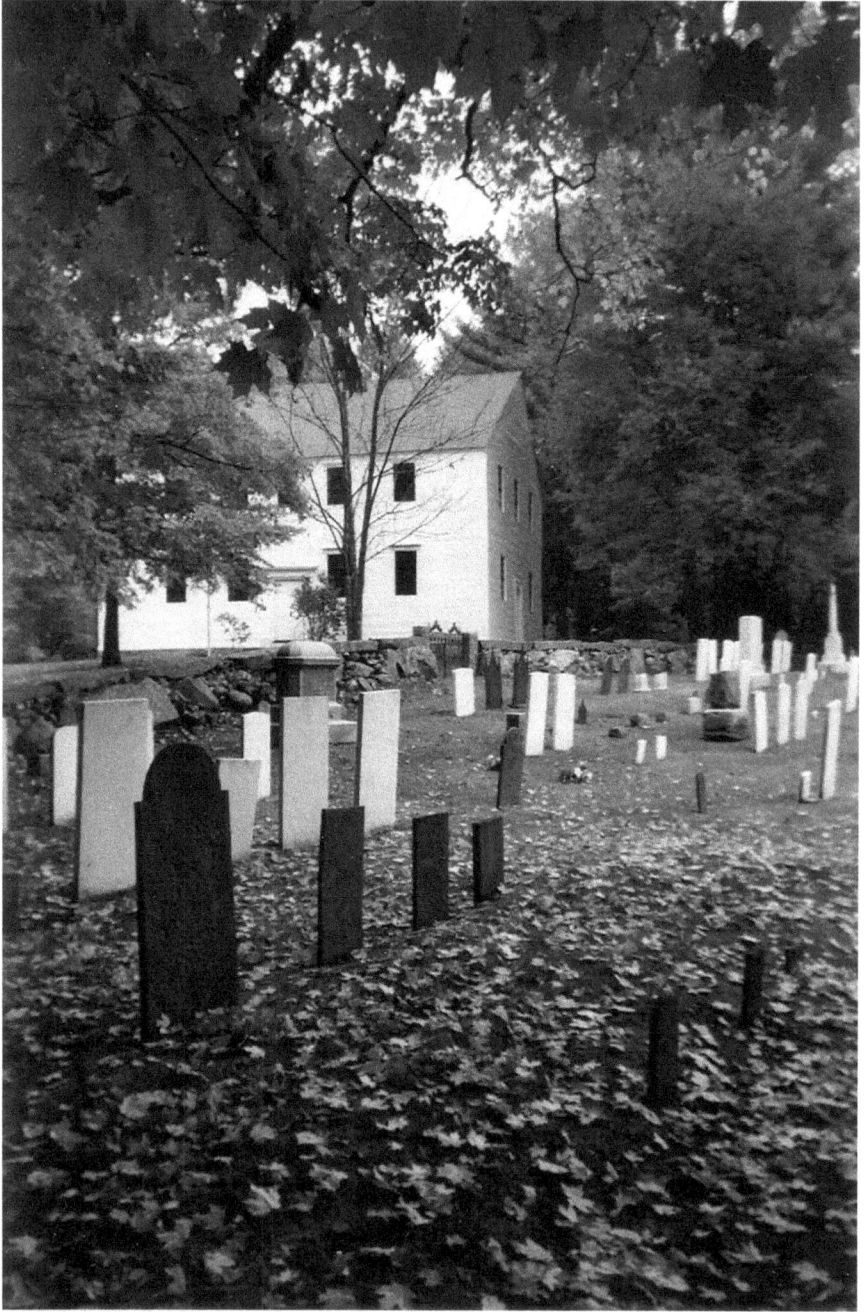

The meetinghouse in which Reverend John Page preached, Hawke (now Danville), New Hampshire. Built in 1755, it is the oldest in New Hampshire surviving in its original condition. *Photograph by author.*

status or even the minister. If she went public with it, she would not only ruin her own reputation but would stand to bring him down as well.

For speculative purposes, let us consider the possibility that the father was someone like Hawke's Reverend John Page. John Page had been called to minister to the little town of Hawke, New Hampshire, in 1763. The town's offer was generous. It included monetary compensation in addition to a house, land and firewood.[62] In Hawke, as in most frontier villages, the minister was also the most educated person. Reverend Page had graduated from Harvard, where he achieved notoriety as a diarist and an avid "frolicker" (partygoer).[63]

We learn from the history of Hawke that Page was in charge of education as well as religion, and therefore he would have been the one who supervised Ruth's work.[64] He also might have enjoyed the company of a literate woman of the same age. Although he was married and dutifully recorded the births of his own children about every eighteen months, one can imagine Ruth, a woman of good family and education, being attractive to and attracted by a man of his education and influence. If so, and if she were perhaps in love with him, she would have preferred to settle things quietly and privately. Many "ifs," to be sure, but this would hardly be the first time that a respectable woman had been impregnated by a man of substance.

Goody Mary Rolfe of Newbury was faced with this choice in 1663 when the local doctor, Henry Greenland, called on her while her husband was away. She claimed that he forced himself on her when she let him step in out of the cold. She feared that her case would not stand up in court because of his prominence: "[H]e is in credit in the town, some take him to be godly and say he hath grace in his face: it is said he is in credit with those in authority in the country…and what [can] such a poor young woman as I do in such a case."[65]

The option of an abortion by ingesting herbal "remedies" that might bring on a miscarriage was risky business. The herbs used, particularly pennyroyal, could be harmful, even fatal, to the woman. If a woman chose to go through with a pregnancy, there was always the possibility of placing it in the home of a childless couple or perhaps a family member willing to assume responsibility for its care and upbringing.

It is also important to remember that unwed women who had some status and education would have had a more difficult time dealing with the stigma and disgrace of an unexpected pregnancy than a lower-class woman whose reputation might be less circumspect. Possibly this was part of Ruth's dilemma and decision not to name the father. Would the court even believe her word over that of a man of good standing and "untarnished" reputation? It seems unlikely in the eighteenth century. She would have had to go public, risking her reputation and his: she would jeopardize her teaching career; if he were married, he would be accused of adultery and publically punished; and if he were single, both would be accused of fornication and suffer a public whipping. Better to avoid the conflict, not to ruin a man's reputation and to handle it among the family and friends. Far better to retreat quietly to another town, have the baby and decide how to continue after the birth.

Chapter 7

South Hampton Summer

Redeem the misspent life that's past,
Live each day as it were thy last.
Then of thy talents take great care,
For the last day thyself prepare.[66]
—1767

The town of South Hampton, New Hampshire, originally part of Amesbury and Salisbury, Massachusetts, was incorporated in 1742 as one of the new towns resulting from the establishment of the 1741 boundary line that permanently settled the ongoing border dispute between the Province of Massachusetts and the Province of New Hampshire.

Leaving the busy highways along the populated coastal plain, the road to South Hampton ascends into the rural beauty of heavily forested hills to arrive at a picture-perfect New England town. The town green is fronted by church and cemetery and bordered by the whitewashed buildings of the town hall and library. Driving north out of town, past the old town cemetery, several colonial homes hug the highway. One of these is the old Currier home, built by and for brothers Reuben and Henry Currier. The two identical sides share a common staircase in the front and an enormous kitchen with a walk-in fireplace at the back. There the two brothers had lived, married and raised their children.

The Reuben and Henry Currier house, where Ruth was purportedly staying when she gave birth. *Photograph by author.*

A short distance away, on the other side of the Currier driveway, the purported cellar hole of the Clough barn can be identified as a shadowy indentation long since filled with brambles, poison ivy, sumac and saplings. Here, in this shallow that still seems to hold grief like a cup, the final chapters of Ruth's story began.

Sometime in the spring of 1768, the pregnant Ruth arrived in the small town of South Hampton, New Hampshire, and according to local history took up residence in the Currier home on today's Main Street. While Sandown history suggests that she stayed with relatives of Sandown's town clerk Reuben Clough, my research into the genealogy of Ruth's grandmother, Lydia Challis, shows that it was more likely that she stayed with the Curriers. Abraham Morrill married Elizabeth Sargent (Lydia's aunt, Ruth's great-aunt). Two of their daughters, Elizabeth and Phebe Morrill, married Henry and Reuben Currier, respectively.[67] These women would have been Ruth's distant cousins, and it seems logical that she would have stayed with them. Reuben's widow, Phebe, had died in 1766, and their married son, Reuben Jr., occupied that side of the house with his wife, Elizabeth.[68] They had a son born in late May 1768, and perhaps

Ruth was able to help the young couple with housework and sewing. The significance of the Currier-Morrill-Blay connection becomes clearer when witnesses are called to testify at Ruth's trial.

Ruth would have been around six months pregnant by the time she came to South Hampton. During the cold winter months, the heavy layers of clothing would have disguised her condition, but by March or April deception would have been more difficult. During the eighteenth century, it would have been rare for women in rural areas to have specially made maternity clothing. Women simply let out the stays in their existing underclothing and adjusted the waistline of overskirts.

An eighteenth-century "maternity" gown. Note the expandable lacings. *Courtesy of the Colonial Williamsburg Foundation*

For many women, the birthing process was social, even celebratory. The midwife would be summoned, as well as a number of female neighbors and friends, and they would take care of the housework and meal preparation, as well as attend the laboring woman. Sometimes "groaning cake" was made during the final phase of labor, and "groaning beer" was brewed.[69]

This would not be the case for Ruth. While it seems nearly impossible that some of the women of the house, as well as neighboring women, would not be aware of Ruth's pregnancy, as far as can be determined Ruth gave birth alone on the night of June 10, 1768.

In a cruel irony, the baby girl was born on her mother's own birthday. According to Ruth's later testimony, a couple of falls had brought on a premature birth, and the child was stillborn. If she had produced but one witness to testify that the child was stillborn, there would have been no suspicion of infanticide. This again suggests that she gave birth alone. Had the story ended there, it would be tragically sad but not life-altering. That was not to be. For whatever reason, Ruth hid the infant's lifeless body under the floorboards of the Clough barn located at the edge of the Currier property. This would seem to give more credence to the belief that she gave birth alone and hastily hid the body there, perhaps planning to bury it more properly when she had recovered from a difficult birth endured under such primitive conditions.

Ruth had little time to recuperate from her trauma. Four days later, on June 14, 1768, five-year-old Betsey Pettingill was accompanying her uncle Benjamin on a trip north to the frontier town of Salisbury, New Hampshire. On the way, they stopped at the Currier home to pay a visit. It was a warm June day, and while the adults socialized, the children played outside. Always an inviting place, the coolness of the barn must have been especially tempting. The loose floorboards aroused their curiosity, and upon lifting them up they discovered the body of an infant.

Betsey's horror was surpassed only by the guilt she later felt about the consequences of their discovery. Eventually, she grew up, married Joel Eastman of Salisbury (New Hampshire) and lived a long and prosperous life. However, the memory of Ruth's fate, and her own part in it, haunted her throughout her 105 years on this earth. She even named one of her children Ruth, possibly in memory of Miss Blay. The impact of her discovery is faithfully recorded in Eastman genealogy:

An Eighteenth-Century New Hampshire Tragedy

When quite young she rode from her home, in Rockingham County, to Salisbury, on a pillion, with her uncle. She was one of a number of young girls who discovered the lifeless body of an infant under a loose floor in a building in South Hampton, connected with the schoolroom where Ruth Blay was teaching. She was then about five years of age. Miss Blay was arrested, tried, and convicted for concealing the death of an infant child...The fact that the discovery was made by Betsey and her schoolmates, in consequence of which Miss Blay was exposed, tried and executed, cast a gloom over Mrs. Eastman's whole subsequent life, and in her later years she often referred to her knowledge of and connection with that melancholy affair, dwelling upon it with much sadness, and exhibiting great feeling and a spirit of compassion for the unfortunate victim...She always had a lurking suspicion that Miss Blay was wrongfully executed...and although at that time her age was under the bounds of responsibility, she felt shocked at having contributed to the death of one who might have been "more sinned against than sinning."[70]

Once the children reported their find, little time was wasted in conducting an investigation into the circumstances of the infant's death. Although childbirth was the province of women, an infant's suspicious death was in the hands of men. On that same day, Philips White, one of the provincial justices of the peace, delivered to Isaac Brown, constable of South Hampton, a warrant for the arrest of Ruth Blay. Consequently, the coroner, Samuel Folsom, gathered sixteen "reputable men" from the town to participate in an inquisition on the infant's body. The all-male "jury" was charged with determining how the baby met its death. After meeting with the coroner, they drafted and affixed their signatures to the following:

"Inquisition on the Body of a Child supposed of Ruth Blay"
An inquisition Indented taken at South Hampton June 14, 1768

Within the said Province of New Hampshire the fourteenth day of June in the eighth year of his Majesty's Reign George the Third by the Grace of God of Great Britain France and Ireland King Defender of the Faith etc. before Samuel Folsom Esq. Coroner of our said Lord the King within the province aforesaid upon view of the body of a female child then and there being dead by the oath of Benjamin Clough, Samuel Fifield, William Rowell, Joseph Eastman, Moses French, Jeremiah Currier, Samuel Quimbe, Prince

63

The signatures on the inquisition upon the body of the infant, noting (in a paragraph immediately above their signatures) their belief that the child had met its death by violence. Blay case. *Courtesy of the New Hampshire Division of Archives and Record Management.*

Flanders, Moses Hoyt, Stephen Rogers, John Tappan, Onesiphorus Page, James French, Reuben Currier, John Morrill and William Graves, good and lawful men of South Hampton aforesaid within the province afore sd who being charged and sworn to enquire for our Lord the King when & by what means & how the said child came to its death, upon their oath, do say that on the fourteenth day of this instant June one thousand seven hundred and sixty-eight the said child was found dead in the barn of one Benjamin Clough of the aforesd South Hampton supposed to be born of the body of one Ruth Blay in said town and it appears to us of the Jury that the child came to its death by violence.[71]

It is important to understand that the men who performed this inquisition on the four-day-old body of an infant female would likely not have been able to differentiate between the bruising caused during the difficult birth of a premature stillborn and that of an infant who had "come to its death by violence."

That evening, in accordance with the law, the coroner sent for Abiah Cooper, midwife, to examine Ruth Blay and determine whether she had lately been delivered of a child. Abiah confirmed what had been suspected and possibly known by some present. Abiah would later be required to appear in Superior Court to give her testimony.[72]

From here, things progressed quickly. The justice of the peace ordered Constable Brown to bring Blay before other justices for further examination. Until June 18, Blay was kept under guard at the constable's home, where three justices questioned her further. Brown's wife was one of a jury of women sworn to search Ruth's person. Then, Constable Brown was ordered to transport the accused to the provincial jail in Portsmouth.

To suffer so much mental, emotional and physical anguish in the short span of one week must have overwhelmed Ruth. She became ill, and Dr. Josiah Bartlett was summoned to tend to her. It would seem apparent that she must have been very ill if his services were required, as it would have been more customary to have a midwife or local herbalist minister to a woman recently delivered of child. Dr. Josiah Bartlett, a man about Ruth's own age, was a rising star in the town of Kingston and eight years later would become one of the signers of the Declaration of Independence. It was Dr. Bartlett who would decide when Ruth was well enough to be taken to Portsmouth and who would also be called to testify at her trial.[73]

Ruth remained under guard in South Hampton for thirty-five more days. For twenty of these days, she was "Confined a Prisoner" at the home of Benjamin Clough. This is recorded in Benjamin's request to the assembly for reimbursement for his troubles, which was granted in 1769.[74] Whether she received any legal advice or the comfort and consolation of friends and family during her time under house arrest is unknown. One can imagine how alone this woman must have felt. Perhaps she was even shunned. Surely she was aware of the law and the possible end result, yet nothing is on record until July 19, when she was finally conveyed to Portsmouth, handed over to the provincial authorities and settled into the jail on Prison Lane to await trial.

Although much of the cleared land of 1768 is again covered by forests, anyone driving along that road now will pass homes that Ruth, too, must

Dr. Josiah Bartlett,
who tended the
ailing Ruth and
gave evidence at her
trial. He became
one of the signers
of the Declaration
of Independence.
*Courtesy of the New
Hampshire Historical
Society.*

have passed as she was transported to the jail by Isaac Brown and an unidentified man and woman. The land is beautiful and rolling, alternating between ridges of high ground and marshy lowlands. Some of the old names still appear on mailboxes and business signs: French, Clough, Currier and Eastman. The beauty of the landscape is marred only by imagining what Ruth must have felt as she was conveyed to a dismal cell in the Portsmouth jail. It's impossible not to wonder whether she took in the sights and sounds of nature as the wagon rumbled along the Exeter road, wondering whether this might be the last time she would take pleasure in such things.

Chapter 8

PORTSMOUTH

Summer of 1768

External Pomp and Visible Success
Sometimes contributes to Our Happiness
But that which makes us Genuine and Refined
A Good Conscience and a Soul Resigned.[75]
—1792

It is doubtful that Ruth had ever been to Portsmouth before. The sights and sounds of the largest and wealthiest town in the province must have seemed quite foreign to the rural schoolteacher. The provincial capital contained some five thousand souls and was the seat of not only the provincial government and court system but also of merchant wealth. A busy port for trade with England and the West Indies, Portsmouth in 1768 was run by wealthy merchants who were friends, relatives or appointees of Governor John Wentworth, who had just succeeded his uncle Benning Wentworth in 1767. Benning's tenure was threatened by increasing displeasure with the manner in which he ruled: appointing relatives to high positions; reserving acreage for himself and the Church of England in 120 town grants; waffling on requests from the assembly for division of the province into counties; and being the royal symbol for recent British taxation laws whether he agreed with them or not.

Governor John Wentworth, who would sign three reprieves for Ruth. *Courtesy of the Portsmouth Athenaeum.*

The governor's appointees, whether related to him or not, were men of wealth and influence who curried favor with the royalist government and garnered political appointments thereby. It is important to remember that most Portsmouth citizens, who lived in the provincial political and judicial center, wished to remain loyal to the mother country but also resented the political restrictions imposed by England, whether through taxation or political appointments. Certainly, patriotic fervor was beginning to increase, but dissent from British rule was less pronounced in Portsmouth than in the rural frontier towns. The shipbuilding business, the West Indies trade and the mast trade flourished, as did the businesses that supported these.

Political unrest was disruptive to these businesses that were the source of their wealth. All persons, regardless of political or religious differences, felt taxation by the Crown to help defray the expenses of the recent wars was excessive. When the Stamp Act of 1765 was repealed in 1767, there was great celebration in Portsmouth—but out of gratitude to the British lords who had succeeded in persuading Parliament to repeal the act, not because the majority desired independence from the mother country. However, when the equally repressive Townshend Acts of 1768 followed, they were met with protests against such taxation without representation in Parliament.

England during this pre-revolutionary decade was experiencing a crisis of confidence in its own government. Election fraud, bribery and government corruption in general threatened the British constitution and the precepts on which it was written. Governor John Wentworth's arrival in 1767 on the heels of the Stamp Act's repeal was much anticipated. His gubernatorial appointment was favorably viewed by the majority, and he was warmly welcomed by Portsmouth citizens. In a letter written by the wife of Reverend Browne, Anglican minister of Queen's Chapel in Portsmouth, she shares the news of his arrival with her daughter and son-in-law: "Mark Wentworth's son John is expected soon from England to be our Governor to the Great Mortification of the old one."[76] The "old one" to whom she refers is, of course, Benning Wentworth who, after twenty-five years of royal favor, was meeting with opposition from the assembly and had been forced to resign. "The old one" had also committed the scandalous act of marrying his twenty-year-old servant girl, Martha Hilton!

Although Wentworth's rule succeeded in expanding and securing New Hampshire's borders, creating new roads and bringing a degree of prosperity to the area, the conflicts that were to blossom into the American Revolution

In his entries for the year 1768, Lane noted simply "Ruth Blay hanged" but also noted growing concern over British taxes and British regiments in Boston.

1768.

had the year past not a hard Winter
month of Febr. verry warme for
- Season; but Colder in March.
had a pretty good midling Crop of Hay
retty good English Corn, but a Thin
? of Indian; it being backward it
+ Tho't there would be hardly any
the begining of Sept. but it was better
u Expectation: & is Sold for 3 or 4 ⅌ Bushd.
the fall & Winter. Hay about 40/ a Load
f plenty at 3 & 4/ old Tenr. ⅌lb   7th Day.
re is much Uneasiness & Trouble in
Land by reason of Duty Laid on glass
Paper &c and a fleet & army of
gulars Sent over to keep orders &
ng us to Subjection.
eneral time of Health & plenty the
r past

Built a Meeting House this year.

were already underway. Submission to a tyrannical government was considered a crime against the greater principle of liberty, so whether this was expressed in repressive taxes or ecclesiastical favoritism, the authority of the British rule in America was challenged. The line between protection and oppression of British colonial subjects was blurred, and liberty hung in the balance.

In October 1768, four regiments of British infantry arrived in Boston to keep the peace. The combination of Stamp Act riots, circulated letters expressing a threat to liberty and assaults against customs officials had all contributed to the belief of colonial governors that extra policing was necessary. These regiments were clearly a standing army, not just garrisoned troops there to protect the colonists, and the resentment and fear of the colonists increased.

Samuel Lane of Stratham expresses this in his diary for the year 1768: "There is much uneasiness & trouble in the Land by reason of Dutys laid on glass tea paper etc. and a fleet & army of regulars sent over to keep order and bring us to Subjection."[77]

In Portsmouth, New Hampshire, but a short forty-five miles from Boston, Governor John Wentworth found himself uncomfortably caught between appeasing an elected assembly that reflected the needs of his constituency and paid his salary and a British royal government that lacked a true understanding of the new world, was itself under attack and relied on his loyalty. This conflict, I believe, was played out in Ruth's trial and conviction.

Such was the climate in the Portsmouth that greeted Ruth Blay when she arrived in July 1768. This was the justice system, and these were the men, that would hear her case and determine her fate. The women of Portsmouth, those of good reputation and some power, would likely have heard of Ruth's trial and may have known about her case but were shielded from its details by the men in their lives who would have thought it improper to discuss a woman of tarnished reputation on trial for obvious sexual misconduct as well as concealment, which to many implied infanticide. Still it begs the question: did none of them feel any sympathy for or kinship with this condemned woman?

To understand what eighteenth-century women in Ruth's position faced when found guilty of concealment and/or infanticide, it is worth taking time to trace the history of the penal code itself regarding this criminal act and explore its interpretation through a few cases that preceded Ruth's trial. It raises interesting questions as to why Ruth's case ended as it did. We shall briefly leave the unfortunate Ruth entering Portsmouth on a warm July day en route to the provincial jail on Prison Lane.

Chapter 9

POLITICS AND PENAL CODES

*Be not wise
In thy own eyes,
Be just and wise
And virtue prize.*[78]
—1724

Almost thirty years earlier, on a frosty late December morning in 1739, two frightened, condemned women woke in the old prison on King's Way in the provincial capitol of Portsmouth, New Hampshire. Both women were tried for and convicted of the crime of concealment of a bastard child, whether it was born dead or alive. The penalty was death by hanging.

There were three major parishes in Portsmouth including the Anglican Queen's Chapel. The latter was attended by most of the wealthy loyalists—among the communicants were the Wentworths, of course; Wyseman Claggett; Thomas Atkinson; and Sheriff Thomas Packer. The other parishes, the South Church and the North Church, were Congregational churches that had once been joined but had separated over a disagreement as to the location of the meetinghouse.

After attending to their dress, the two women were escorted from the jail to their respective houses of worship to hear sermons meant to remind them of their crimes and better prepare them to meet their deaths. Widow

Sarah Simpson, about twenty-seven, was from Durham and had been put out to service in Portsmouth at an early age. She attended South Church, where the Reverend William Shurtleff preached from Luke 23:42. Penelope Kenny, an Irish servant girl of the "Romish Religion," heard the Reverend Arthur Brown of Queen's Chapel preach from Proverbs 22:6.[79]

Shurtleff's sermon addressed both the pathos of the women's condition and the inherent danger of tolerating such deviations from both the law and the church. In *The Faith and Prayer of a Dying Malefactor*, Shurtleff references the crucifixion of Christ and the thieves crucified on either side of him—one mocked Jesus and the other rebuked the mocker and begged forgiveness.

The minister then proceeded to warn of the horrors of hell, extol the glories of heaven and pray that the "Widow Woman Sarah Simpson," who had seriously neglected her faith but who had enjoyed a renewal of the same while imprisoned, would find mercy from her redeemer. She had, in fact, dictated a paper to be read the previous Sunday beseeching the parishioners to pray for her.

Also mentioned by Shurtleff was the occasion when some "indiscreet" persons tried to convince them they did not deserve to suffer the severe punishment and attempted to conspire with them to escape from prison. Although the planned escape never happened, Shurtleff laments that it "diverted their Minds" from working on their salvation. Having been imprisoned since their August sentencing, one can imagine such a diversion might have been most welcome![80]

Accompanied by their ministers, the women walked to the gallows, which had been erected about a mile outside the town's center, at the corner where today's South Street and Middle Road meet. According to Shurtleff's published account of the event, both women behaved in a penitent manner, Sarah almost beatific in demeanor. "She all the way discover'd an uncommon Composure of Mind, and gave very pertinent Answers to the Questions that were put to her."[81]

At the gallows, each was allowed a final statement before the noose was placed around her neck and she was swung off. Sarah's mentions "several Things that were Matter of Grief and Bitterness to her, as, That she had been so forgetful of God in her Childhood and Youth, and pass'd away her early Days in light and wicked Company."[82] She continues on in that vein, chastising herself for not having honored the Sabbath and misusing opportunities in her later years when she was employed by practicing

Christians, ending by cautioning young persons to live, marry and raise children in the faith.

Penelope also had read a similar statement before her execution. Shurtleff mentions the uncommon number of spectators present and the uncommon concern visible in all and prays that the impressions made on them may "have an happy Effect that not only such as law, but that all such as hear may fear: That those who are in their younger Years would flee youthful Lusts… shun the Sin which has been the Occasion of bringing these Persons to this untimely End."[83] Such evidence of the erosion of morals had necessitated taking even greater care in writing the execution sermons for these women before publishing them to make them available to the general public.

Following the hanging, the women were buried under the street. It is somehow comforting to know that Ruth is at least buried in what is now "hallowed" ground, unlike her sad predecessors Penelope and Sarah.

Ironically, their crimes might never have been discovered had not a third infant been discovered drowned in a well in Portsmouth. Penelope and Sarah were known to have been pregnant, and so were immediately suspect, yet the mother of the child in the well was never positively identified and remained, as Shurtleff mentions in his sermon, "one among us, thro' whose Means these Persons have been remarkably detected, that is equally & it may be much more heinously, guilty in the Sight of God."[84]

The *Boston Post Boy* carried the story on August 20, 1739:

> *Last Saturday Morning was found Dead in a Well here, a Female infant lately born, and supposed to be murdered and warrants being issued out by His Majesty's Justices of the Peace to Search for the Mother…and in the Afternoon a Widow Woman named Sarah Simpson who had been Suspected Some Time before to have been with Child, was apprehended and charged with being the Mother of the Child found in the Well, which she denyed: but at the same Time said she would go and show where she had buried her Child, and accordingly went with the Constable who apprehended her and dug up her Child…being buried about four Inches under-Ground by the River-side…and on Sunday last in the Afternoon and Irish Woman Servant of Dr. Joseph Franklin of this Town was apprehended as a Suspected Person…but She denied the Child found in the Well was Hers…however said at last that she might have done something bad…whereupon she was committed to Prison…and then she owned that*

she was alone delivered of a Male Child alive the Wednesday morning before; that she put it alive into a tub in her Master's Cellar and then left it 'till Friday Night following, when she threw it into the River…Upon which some are of the Opinion, that there is another Mother yet to be found for the Child taken out of the Well; others think she is already found.[85]

Neither admitted nor was convicted of infanticide. Neither named the father, probably because it would only have been useful had the child lived. This was a "woman's crime," and establishing paternity would have served no purpose. It would not save either woman from being convicted of *concealment*. There was a narrow line between concealment and infanticide, and unless at least one person could testify that the child was born dead, or probably born dead because of a preexisting condition, a woman must be able to defend herself against both crimes. The punishment for conviction of either crime was clear: death by hanging. The burden of proving good intent was on the accused.

While Ruth's case is in some ways similar to that of Sarah and Penelope, it is clear that by the second half of this century perception of the adopted British law had changed, the fervor of several spiritual "awakenings" had somewhat abated, religious diversification was well established and the patriotic spirit of revolution was brewing. Another significant difference between the first and second half of the century is that the horrific impact of the throat distemper on the population of children was no longer in the forefront of people's minds. The loss of so many children merely two years prior to the trial of Sarah and Penelope, coupled with the spiritual revival of that period, must have made them appear far less sympathetic figures.

By mid-century, the wisdom of such severely cruel and gender-specific punishment was being questioned. The acts and laws passed by the colonial assemblies and enforced by the provincial court system were basically the British laws of the mother country, with some adaptation to circumstances in the New World. The modern law regarding infanticide, a term not even used during the colonial period, had its roots in these early laws. These British laws were first formulated and passed in a 1624 English statute that reads almost word for word like the New Hampshire law passed over one hundred years later. In 1759, the New Hampshire General Assembly passed the "Acts and Laws of His Majesty's Province of New Hampshire." These contained the law that would be applied in all the concealment/infanticide

TO THE

Chriſtian Reader.

THE Women, that were lately executed at *Portſmouth*, were condemn'd
by a Law, which I think proper to
recite, omitting the Preamble, that it
may be better known in all Families
that ſhall have the following Sermon.

" An Act to prevent the deſtroying and mur-
" dering of Baſtard Children.

" *Be it enacted by the Governour, Council and Re-*
" *preſentatives conven'd in General Aſſembly, and by*
" *the Authority of the ſame,* That if any Woman be
" deliver'd of any Iſſue of her Body, Male or
" Female, which if it were born alive, ſhould by
" Law be a Baſtard, and that ſhe endeavour pri-
" vately, either by drowning or ſecret burying
" thereof, or any other Way, either by herſelf,
" or by the procuring of others ſo to conceal the
" Death thereof, that it may not come to Light,
" whether it were born alive or not, but be con-
" ceal'd ; in every ſuch Caſe the Mother ſo of-
" fending ſhall ſuffer Death, as in Caſe of Mur-
" der; except ſuch Mother can make Proof, by
" one Witneſs at the leaſt, the Child, whoſe
" Death was by her ſo intended to be conceal'd,
" was born Dead."
The Execution of the ſaid Women drew together a vaſt Concourſe of People, and probably
the greater, becauſe theſe were the firſt Executions that ever were ſeen in this Province : For,
altho'

The law regarding concealment repeated in the preface to the Reverend
Shurtleff's execution sermon for Sarah Simpson. *Courtesy of the New
Hampshire Historical Society.*

cases during this period. It had existed also in 1739, and Shurtleff himself copies it word for word at the beginning of his sermon.

In the published laws of 1759 appears "An Act to Prevent the Destroying and Murdering of Bastard Children." The law itself is prefaced by the justification for it and reads as follows:

> *Whereas many lewd women that have been delivered of bastard children, to avoid their shame, and to escape punishment, do secretly bury or conceal the death of their children, and after, if the child be found dead, the said woman to allege that the said Child was born dead: Whereas it falleth out sometimes, (altho' hardly it is to be proved) that the said child or children were murdered by the said women their lewd mothers, or by their assent or procurement:*

> *Be it therefore Enacted by the Governor, Council, and Representatives, convened in General Assembly, and by the Authority of the same:*

> *That if any woman be delivered of any issue of her body, male or female, which if it were born alive should by law be a bastard, and they endeavor privately, either by drowning, or secret burying thereof, that it may not come to light, whether it was born alive or not, but be concealed; in every such case the mother so offending shall suffer death, as in case of murder, except such mother can make proof, by one witness at the least, that the child whose death was by her so intended to be concealed, was born dead.*[86]

Statistically, the indictment and conviction rate for this crime in both England and New England experienced rises and falls. It rose throughout the first half of the eighteenth century, and then began to wane again.[87] Clearly, it represented a reflection of the perceived immorality of the time, and social or political unrest seems to have paralleled that perception. Notice that the very language in the preface assumes the impropriety of the woman; it is not modified at all by the circumstance of the pregnancy. She is *presumed* to be a "lewd" woman.

The laws regarding fornication and bastardy mandated much less severe punishment. Fornication was punishable by whipping and fines to both parties; bastardy, if the father was named during the woman's travail and this was witnessed by midwife or friend, was punishable by financial responsibility for the child and/or imprisonment until he could assure the town that he would be financially responsible for said child.[88]

In provincial New Hampshire, as in other colonies, these laws were tested. During the second half of the eighteenth century, societal order was indeed being challenged on all sides. It is obvious that whenever the established order is threatened—be it politically, legally, morally, spiritually or socially—the application of the established controls is more stringent. Certainly this was true in 1739 for Sarah and Penelope with the throat distemper and the Great Awakening fresh in people's minds, and it would be true again in the pre-revolutionary unrest of 1768.

Ruth was not the first to be indicted and tried for the crime of concealment and/or infanticide after the 1739 hangings of Penelope and Sarah. By the middle of the eighteenth century, juries seemed more reluctant to prosecute to the full extent of the existing law in cases of infanticide, and several different kinds of pleas were being made by the defense. The "benefit-of-linen" plea first successfully used in England simply proved that a woman had fully intended to birth and keep an infant by virtue of showing the jury clothes that she had made in preparation for its birth. Another common plea was "want-of-help," in which the accused could show that the infant's death was an accident due to ignorance and unintentional negligence. Impairment of the mother's physical and mental health by illness, falls or mental deficiencies was another possible avenue to a "not guilty" verdict.[89]

Who were some of the other women who had been indicted and had successfully defended themselves in New Hampshire and other New England provinces, and how did they do so? To answer, it is helpful to look beyond New Hampshire to neighboring Massachusetts and Connecticut. In their study of infanticide during this period, *Murdering Mothers: Infanticide in England and New England 1558–1803*, Hoffer and Hull state that in Massachusetts after 1730 only four out of thirty indicted for infanticide were convicted.[90] Word of these new pleas had been disseminated and must clearly have been known by Ruth, who in her written declaration mentions that she had made clothing for the infant (benefit of linen) and also describes two falls (physical health; miscarriage; and stillborn) prior to delivery.

In New Hampshire, two other cases of concealment and possible infanticide can be found in the superior court records of this period. In 1763, Mary Flood, of no fixed town, was arraigned for the crime of concealment of an infant in the town of Stevenstown (now Salisbury); pleading "not guilty," she put herself upon the country for trial. In the court record, it rather summarily states that upon both the attorney for the king and attorney for the defendant being heard on the evidence, the case was turned over to the jury, who pronounced Mary "not guilty."

There are written witness statements from two women, Dorothy Sanborn and Elizabeth Brown, stating that on the night of September 30 Mary had gone alone to the side of the barn of one John Brown and delivered a baby. Elizabeth, wife of John Brown, testified that during that day before the birth, Mary was taken very sick with vomiting and was afraid she "like to have the bloody purging and said she could not stay in the house," but Elizabeth insisted that she come inside and put her to bed, as she was afraid that Mary would hurt her child with the severe vomiting. Later, Elizabeth, who lay beside Mary, said "she could no longer feel the child move inside Mary and was afraid it was dead before it was born." Her neighbor, Dorothy Sanborn, confirmed that by saying Elizabeth had told her that when she lay with Mary in the bed she at first felt Mary Flood's baby alive; later that night she checked several times and felt no life.[91] We have these written witness statements because these women were unable to travel to Portsmouth to give evidence in person.

In the inquisition, it further notes that Mary put the infant into a "woman pocket"—a type of gathered pocket worn between the outer dress and petticoat—and carried it to the bank of the river, covering it with soil from the riverbank. Mary claimed that the child was stillborn, and the members of the inquisition could find no mark of violence on the body. Clearly, it was the combination of the female witnesses confirming a stillbirth and the men observing no marks of violence on the body that saved Mary's life. Although still guilty of concealment, the jury in the superior court acquitted her.[92]

In the year 1765, another case came before the superior court involving a young woman named Rachel Eaton of Hampton Falls. Rachel was accused of murdering her male bastard child by leaving the infant in a field "far from habitation" without clothing and in inclement weather. Rachel, too, pleaded "not guilty" and put herself on trial. Witnesses having been heard, the jury retired and returned a verdict of "not guilty." Rachel, too, was discharged—a free woman.[93]

These trials make it even more difficult to understand Ruth's case—were the courts and juries simply unwilling to pardon another woman for fear of taking these crimes too lightly and encouraging loose morals? Was Rachel, perhaps, considered mentally deficient and unable to understand the consequence of her actions? If Ruth had been the first of these women charged instead of the third, would it have made a difference? Had the climate in America changed sufficiently that Wentworth decided not to grant Ruth a pardon as an expression of British control?

Yet another interesting case that was tried before the superior court in 1763 involved a woman from Portsmouth named Margaret Smallcorn. Unlike the others, the charges against Margaret were for the crime of adultery by repeatedly having consensual "Carnal Copulation" with one John Collier over a period of time of approximately one year, thereby violating the covenant of her marriage "to the Evil Example of all others." Margaret was found guilty and punished in the following manner:

> *The Court do order that the said Margaret shall set upon the Gallows, by the Space of one hour, with a Rope about her Neck and the other end cast over the Gallows & in the way to the Common Jail, Shall be Severely whipped ten stripes on her naked Back, & shall forever after wear a Capital Letter A of two Inches Long & Proportionable in bigness cut out in Cloth of a Contrary Colour to her Cloaths & Sewed upon her upper Garment on the Outside of her Arm or on her Back in open View during her abode in this Province & for Cost of Prosecution taxed at the Sum of thirty-two pounds fourteen Shillings standing Committed till Sentence be performed.[94]*

A different crime, certainly, but one demonstrating the prevailing view of women as the protectors of morals, as well as their severe punishment for violating this role. This antiquated law regarding adultery remains on the books in New Hampshire, with a bill being submitted only recently (and facing some opposition!) to repeal it. Although attitudes of juries were changing and though there was a degree of sympathy for these women, particularly those guilty only of concealment, it is clear that in Ruth's case a strict interpretation of the law would take precedence over the more modern trend toward leniency.

If laws are essentially codifications of morality and societal control mechanisms, then Ruth's fate may have been determined less by a belief in her guilt than by the established British rule's need to show firmness and loyalty to the appointed magistrates and, in so doing, uphold the laws that supported order in the community. Certainly, the morals they codified were

Margaret Smallcorn's sentence for adultery: to wear a "Scarlet A" on her clothing for the rest of her time in New Hampshire. Superior Court Records. *Courtesy of the New Hampshire Division of Archives and Record Management.*

religiously based and additionally reflected the culture and politics of the times. Defining "justice" becomes a difficult task when there are oppositional forces within a society, both of which can make a reasonable, rational case to support their viewpoint. These acts were clearly illegal and the punishments legal—but were they "just"?

Chapter 10

King v. Blay

Teach me to feel another's woe
To hide the fault I see
That mercy I to others shew
That mercy shew to me.[95]
−1787

R uth arrived at the relatively new jail on Prison Lane in July 1768. It stood roughly where today's Music Hall stands. Built in 1759, the jail was two stories high and built of "oak timber hewn square and covered with iron bars, well spiked to the timber, and lined with plank."[96] The walls were between eight and ten inches thick, and the jailer's quarters were connected to it. The floor plan of the prison "Proposed to be built in Portsmouth" was discovered in the New Hampshire Division of Archives and Records Management and shows the ordinary cells and the "secure" cells reserved for those accused of capital crimes. We can safely assume that Ruth would have occupied one of these, due to the high-profile nature of her case. Eighteenth-century prisons were bleak, crude places that would make our modern high-security prisons look luxurious. The illustration of a cell in the Old York Gaol from the same time period conveys a good idea of the harshness of the old prisons. Here, Ruth would be housed for some five and a half months, through the oppressive heat of summer and the bone-chilling cold of early winter.

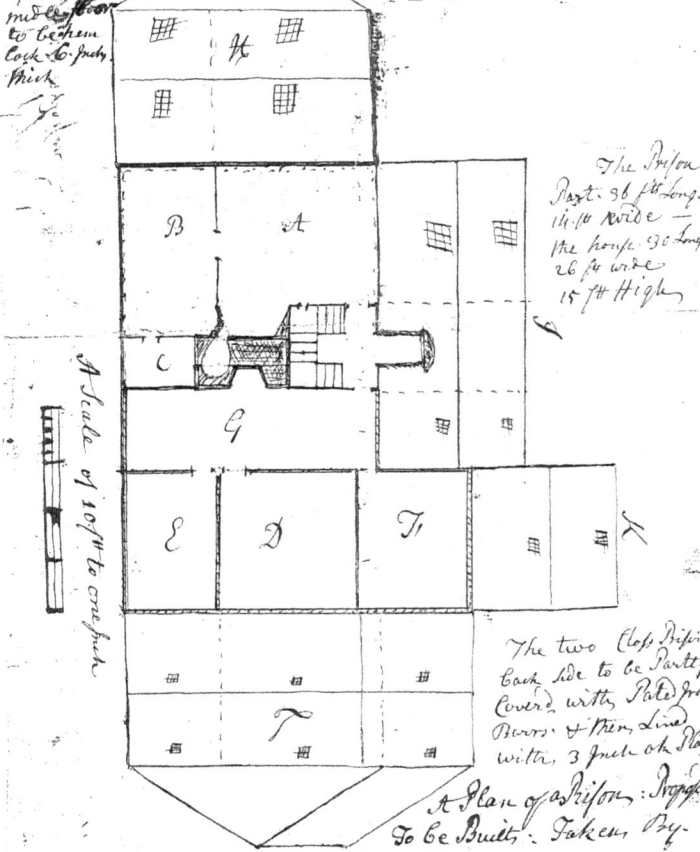

The 1759 plan for a new prison in Portsmouth. One of these cells would have been Ruth's home for some six months, where she was sometimes "bound in chains." *Courtesy of the New Hampshire Division of Archives and Record Management.*

A jail cell in the Old Gaol in York, Maine. This was typical of a cell in eighteenth-century New England jails. *Photograph by Jack Boucher, 1965. Courtesy of the Library of Congress, Historic American Buildings Survey.*

The courthouse where Ruth would appear was located in the west end of the old statehouse. That building was erected in the middle of King Street, now Congress Street, in front of the North Church. The east end of the building served as the province's Assembly House. On August 2, Ruth was "brought a prisoner to the Bar" and arraigned. She pleaded not guilty and put herself "on the Country for Trial."[97] Her trial was adjourned until September 21, one month later. In the interim, about a week before the trial, Ruth's sisters, Mary and Abigail, and Ruth's mother, Lydia, were summoned to appear in court on September 19 "to give Evidence of what you know relating to an action…to Be heard and tried betwixt our Sovereign Lord the King and Ruth Blay."[98] Because all of the witnesses called to testify for and against Ruth appeared in person, we have no written record of their testimony.

The trial of *King v. Blay* began on September 21 with a jury of twelve men sworn in by King's Attorney Wyseman Claggett. Justice Claggett had a reputation for being stern but fair and generally believed in strict adherence to the law. However, in the case of the prosecution of Ruth Blay, he is reported to have opened the trial with an "inflated exordium [apology]...for the enforcement of a statute so abhorrent to every sentiment of humanity call[ing] Heaven to witness that he was discharging a duty that he owed his country, his King, and his God!"[99]

The witnesses were summoned to give testimony, and according to the *New Hampshire Gazette*, "the Trial lasted from Ten o'Clock, A.M. to Six in the afternoon,"[100] when the jury at last retired. The next day, the jury, after "being out almost the whole Night before they were agreed...brought in their verdict."[101] Ruth, found guilty, was legally convicted of the "felony charged against her"—that is, of the "private burial and concealment of her Bastard child at South Hampton...contrary to our Peace, Crown and Dignity and against the Law in such cases made and provided, and to the evil Example of others in the like Case offending."[102]

Sentence was then passed. "By the Consideration of the Justices of our said Superior Court of Judicature, the said Ruth Blay for the Burial and Concealment aforesaid, is condemned to suffer the pains of Death, in hanging by her neck, till her Body be dead."[103] Asked whether she had any legal objection to the sentence, Ruth offered none and was remanded to the custody of Sheriff Thomas Packer, with a date of November 24 being set for the execution. His orders were clear:

> *We Command you therefore that, on Thursday the Twenty fourth day of November, next ensuing Between the hours of Twelve of the Clock at noon and Two of the Clock afternoon, of the same day, you carry the said Ruth Blay from our Gaol in Portsmouth aforesaid, where She now is in your Custody, to the place of Execution in said Portsmouth, and cause her, the said Ruth Blay to be then and there hanged by her neck till her Body be dead. Hereof fail not, and for your so doing this shall be your Sufficient Warrant.*[104]

While this first order fixes the time of execution between the hours of twelve o'clock and two o'clock, subsequent orders following all three reprieves fix the hours between ten o'clock and two o'clock. The importance of this will be seen when the nineteenth- and twentieth-century versions of the Ruth Blay story are reviewed.

The indictment and sentence document from the Superior Court records at the New Hampshire State Archives. *Courtesy of the New Hampshire Division of Archives and Record Managemeny.*

Old North Church, Old Bell Tavern   Old Colonial State House,   Old Pump   Athenaeum,
1712—1854,   1743—1857,   1758—1836,   and Whipping Post   1803,

Postcard showing location and architecture of the Old Assembly House and Court in Portsmouth, New Hampshire. *Courtesy of the Portsmouth Athenaeum.*

How Ruth and her family reacted to the conviction and sentence can only be imagined. Surely they must have heard of the women who had been tried and acquitted in recent years, and the guilty verdict must have come as a shock. Ruth had never denied the concealment, and she was not being tried for anything else, although there were clearly those who thought her guilty of infanticide. Had the jurors read into the testimony of some of her South Hampton neighbors? Had they, the witnesses, misled or misinformed the jurors, leaving some doubt in their minds as to Ruth's character or intent? The testimony of the witnesses is not known, but the seriousness with which some of them took the trial will be challenged by Ruth in her final statement. The long process of appealing for a reprieve must now begin.

Chapter 11

Hope and Despair

Despair of nothing
that you would attain
Unwearied diligence
your point will gain.[105]
−1730

The reprieves Ruth was granted were sought for the purpose of securing more time in which to better prepare herself to face death. There are no known appeals to the court for a new trial based on new evidence. It is not until her written declaration that there is even a hint that she might have better defended herself had she not been advised against using the "benefit of linen" plea.

Having petitioned the governor, Ruth was rewarded on November 23, the day before her execution, when she received the first reprieve from John Wentworth. It reads as follows:

And forasmuch as the said Ruth Blay did humbly supplicate our Mercy for the respiting the Execution of said Sentence some further time, that She might have a better opportunity to prepare for Her Death, She having likewise expressed a sorrowful and penitent Sense of her said Crime. We did therefore order that the Execution of said Sentence of Death on the

The third and final reprieve from Governor John Wentworth, clearly setting the time of execution between the hours of ten o'clock and two o'clock. *Courtesy of the New Hampshire Archives and Record Management.*

said Ruth Blay should Be respited and deferred till Friday the 9ᵗʰ Day of
December Instant, between the hours of Ten and Two o'Clock in the said
Day and no longer.[106]

Granted two more weeks to live, Ruth must have felt enormous relief, as
well as sheer exhaustion from the anticipation of an answer delivered hours
before her date with death. Apparently, no time was wasted in preparing
yet another request for time, for on December 8 she similarly received from
Governor Wentworth notice that her execution had again been reprieved
until December 24. Again she petitioned the governor, and in what would be
the final week of her life, she was granted a third and final reprieve, setting
a new date, December 30, for her execution.

This was when her luck ran out. Whether she petitioned for yet another
reprieve is not known. If so, the record of it has not survived. In that last
reprieve, the time of execution is clearly set for December 30 between the
hours of ten o'clock and two o'clock.[107]

On the final night of her life, Ruth requested pen and paper to record and
have witnessed a final statement. It is striking when compared to the statements
of Sarah and Penelope. Ruth is an educated woman with a clear sense of what
she did and a clear understanding of the injustice of her sentence.

She not only professes her innocence and says that it is "that knowledge
and God's mercy" on which she will rely, but she also accuses some of
bearing false witness against her. She wished the statement to be published
in the *New Hampshire Gazette* on Friday morning. This was done, and as it was
printed at two o'clock in the morning before the execution took place, there
is no black border or death angel heading. A copy of this original broadside
is located in the holdings of the Harry Houdini Museum at the University
of Texas.

Ruth Blay's final words—indeed the only ones that can be confirmed as
hers—are contained in the written declaration read before three witnesses
on the eve of her execution. The declaration was reprinted as far south as
Philadelphia and New York, after being published as a broadside by the *New*
Hampshire Gazette. As stated, the posthumous reprints are bordered in black,
capped by an angel of death. It is all that we have in her voice:

To the Public. As it is now but a few Hours, before I must exchange this
mortal State, for one that is eternal, it will be no Advantage to me to say any

THE
Declaration and Confeſſion
OF
Ruth Blay,

Who was tried at His Majeſty's Superior Court in Portſmouth, New-Hampſhire, September 21ſt, 1768, for concealing the Birth of her Infant, which was found dead ; and is to be executed this 30th Day of December 1768.

TO THE PUBLIC.

AS it is now but a few Hours, before I muſt exchange this mortal ſtate, for one that is eternal, it will be no Advantage to me to ſay any Thing that is amuſing, trifling, or impertinent, to the numerous Spectators, ſome of whom no Doubt, will come out of Curioſity to ſee the Behaviour of a poor condemn'd Perſon ; others out of Pity and Compaſſion ; but whatever may be their View, I now appear a Spectacle to Angels and Men ; but what are all Things of a temporal Nature to me ?—— Nothing, but GOD in CHRIST, and my own Conſcience are of any Avail with me ;—as to the bleſſed Angels they are Happy beyond the Deſcription of my feeble Pen to deſcribe—As to my Fellow Creatures, we are all upon a Level as to the Mercy of GOD ;—they muſt ſoon follow, though perhaps not in the ſame ignominious Way ; but the Death I am to undergo, is not ſo painful as that my SAVIOUR has undergone before, on whoſe Merits alone I rely for Pardon and Acceptance——Nothing but a Conſciouſneſs of my own Innocence and his Preſence has upheld my drooping Spirits for above five Months, while I have been bound in Chains.——It is now needleſs for me to give a ſhort Hiſtory of my Life, which I had ſome Thought of, and perhaps had I d——e it, though it might ſeem vain in me, would have appeared as circumſpect as ſome of my Accuſers, who have borne FALSE WITNESS againſt me.

Before I enter upon any Particulars relating to my Trial and Condemnation ; I would return my moſt ſincere Thanks to his Excellency the GOVERNOR, for the Reprieves He has already given me from Time to Time, and alſo to the Reverend MINISTERS, who have ſo often viſited me in my Confinement ; and alſo for their good Offices in a more public Way for my Spiritual Advantage.——And am alſo far from Caſting any Reflection on the honourable JUDGES ; as I apprehend the Infatuation muſt lie in ſome of the Witneſſes, and ſome of the Jury ;——

And now for the Truth of what I am going to ſay, I appeal to that GOD before whom I muſt ſhortly appear, and call Heaven and Earth to Witneſs, that though I was with Child, I never had a ſingle Thought of murdering the Infant, which makes me even ſhudder to think that it is poſſible any Mother ſhould be guilty of ſuch Cruelty—and therefore I made Preparation for its Birth, and could now produce the Cloaths and Woman in whoſe keeping they are ; but alaſs ! it is too late ;—and on that unhappy Day when I was delivered, I knew it had not been eight Months from the Time I was with Child, therefore had no Thoughts of being delivered at that Time ; but an unhappy Fall, which I then received, brought on the Birth inſtantly :——

Having alſo had another unhappy Fall about ten Days before, which gave me great Uneaſineſs ; and at which Time I apprehend my Child died ; ſo that the Child was dead born : and to conceal the Shame, I hid it in the beſt Manner I could, and ever after was loath to reveal it, as I imagined no Good could come thereby ; but ſhould have diſcloſed the whole to my Lawyers, had I been adviſed by my Friends not to do it, and thus I have been condemned,—I muſt declare to the laſt that the Witneſſes have miſrepreſented Facts, and ſome of them appeared with Countenances that plainly ſhewed they were unaffected with the Solemnity of the Trial, and fear they as little regarded the Solemnity of an Oath,—The Time being now ſo ſhort, after returning Thanks to all Friends for the Kindneſſes ſhown me, I muſt bid them farewell, and hope no one will caſt any Reflections on my aged Mother, Siſters, and other Relations, on my Account, as my Conſcience is clear with Reſpect to my poor Infant ;—And though I die with a forgiving Spirit as to all my Enemies, but charge the two Women in particular to examine their own Hearts, as they will anſwer it another Day, whether they do not come under the Character of falſe Witneſſes ?—And whether Prejudice, Jealouſy or ſomething elſe has not drove them thus to bear falſe Witneſs againſt me,

Ruth Blay,

PORTSMOUTH - PRISON, December 29th, 1768.
Thurſday Evening eight o'Clock.
☞ The foregoing Declaration was read and ſign'd in Preſence of three Witneſſes, and was deſir'd it might be made public immediately.

Friday Morning two o'Clock, December 30th, 1768, Printed, And to be Sold at the Printing-Office in Portſmouth.

The published broadside *The Declaration and Confession of Ruth Blay.* This copy, headed by the death angel, indicates that it was published after the execution, probably by the *Essex Gazette* in Salem, Massachusetts. *Courtesy of the Peabody Essex Museum, Phillips Library Collection.*

Thing that is amusing, trifling, or impertinent, to the numerous Spectators, some of whom no Doubt, will come out of Curiosity to see the Behavior of a poor condemn'd Person; others out of Pity and Compassion; but whatever may be their View, I now appear a Spectacle to Angels and Men; but what are all things of a temporal Nature to me? —Nothing, but God in Christ, and my own Conscience are of any Avail with me;—As to my Fellow Creatures, we are all upon a Level as to the Mercy of God;—they must soon follow, though perhaps not in the same ignominious Way; but the Death I am to undergo, is not so painful as that my Saviour has undergone before, on whose Merits alone I rely for Pardon and Acceptance—Not but a Consciousness of my own Innocence and his Presence has upheld my drooping Spirits for about five Months, while I have been bound in Chains—It is now needless for me to give a short History of my Life, which I had some Thought of, and perhaps had I done it, though it might seem vain in me, would have appeared as circumspect as some of my Accusers, who have borne FALSE WITNESS against me.

Before I enter upon any particulars relating to my Trial and Condemnation; I would return my most sincere Thanks to his Excellency the GOVERNOR, for the Reprieves He has already given me from Time to Time; and also to the Reverend MINISTERS, who have so often visited me in my Confinement; and also for their good Offices in a more public Way for my Spiritual Advantage,—And am also far from Casting any Reflection on the honourable JUDGES; as I apprehend the Infatuation must lie in some of the Witnesses, and some of the Jury;—

And now for the Truth of what I am going to say, I appeal to the God before whom I must shortly appear, and call Heaven and Earth to Witness, that though I was with Child, I never had a Single Thought of murdering the Infant, which makes me even shudder to think that it is possible any Mother should be guilty of such Cruelty—and therefore I made Preparation for its Birth, and could now produce the Cloaths and Woman in whose keeping they are; but alas! it is too late;—and on that unhappy Day when I was delivered, I knew it had not been eight Months from the Time I was with Child, therefore had not Thoughts of being delivered at that time; but an unhappy Fall which I then received, brought on the Birth instantly:—

Having also had another unhappy Fall about ten Days before, which gave me great Uneasiness; and at which Time I apprehend my Child died; so that the Child was dead born: and to conceal the Shame, I hid it in the best Manner I could, and ever after was loath to reveal it, as I imagined no Good could come thereby; but should have disclosed the whole to my Lawyers, but was advised by my Friends not to do it, and thus I have been condemned.—I must declare to the last that the Witnesses have misinterpreted Facts, and some of them appeared with Countenances that plainly shewed they were unaffected with the Solemnity of the Trial, and fear they as little regarded the Solemnity of an Oath.—The Time being now so short, after returning Thanks to all Friends for the Kindnesses shown me, I must bid them farewell, and hope no one will cast any Reflections on my aged Mother, Sisters and other Relations on my Account, as my Conscience is clear with respect to my poor Infant;—And though I die with a forgiving Spirit as to all my Enemies, but charge the two Women in particular to examine their own Hearts, as they will answer it another Day, whether they do not come under the Character of false Witnesses?—And whether Prejudice, Jealousy or something else has not drove them thus to bear false Witness against me.

Ruth Blay.
PORTSMOUTH PRISON
December 29th, 1768
Thursday Evening eight o'Clock

The foregoing Declaration was read and signed in presence of three Witnesses, and was desir'd
It might be made public immediately.[108]

In this, her only attempt to explain the circumstances that led to the final act of her personal tragedy, Ruth seems to have wanted to accomplish only three things: to pardon her judges; to explain the birth of her stillborn and her decision to conceal it; and to admonish those who she felt had born "false witness" against her, thus swaying the verdict of some members of the jury.

Because of the sudden and unexpected nature of what she describes as a premature birth, there was likely no witness to her travail, no witness to testify whether the child was in fact stillborn. According to law, even one witness who could testify to the fact that the baby was stillborn might have worked to her benefit. Under the circumstances, however, even friends might have remained silent to avoid accusations of complicity.

Certainly, someone knew of her pregnancy, and she leaves no doubt that she was preparing for the child and wanted the child. Her claim to be able to produce the clothes she had prepared for the babe, and the woman in whose care she had left them, was obviously an attempt to invoke the "benefit of linen" plea that had saved others from her fate. She states she had been advised not to bring the clothes and woman as evidence of her good intentions—perhaps ill-advised. In addition, she mentions two falls, accidents that had precipitated an early birth. The first fall she believed had caused the baby's death; the second precipitated a premature birth. This, too, had been used successfully as a defense. Thus it seems clear that in this final declaration of her innocence she is referencing pleas used by others accused of infanticide, concealment or both.

Clearly, she seems most distressed by the two young women whom she accused of not appreciating the seriousness of the trial and also of bearing false witness. Who these women were is open to speculation, but we can speculate that they were the youngest women there, either Benjamin Clough's sisters or Olive, Benjamin's wife. Because Ruth states that had she given a short history of her life—she would have appeared as "circumspect" as some of her accusers—there must have been something in their testimony impugning Ruth's character. Unfortunately, the existing court records do not include any of the witnesses' testimony, positive or negative.

Chapter 12

THE CLOUGH CONNECTION

Consider well some by past days
On former Times reflect
And see if thou in all thy ways
Are truly circumspect.[109]
–1760

In attempting to ascertain the identity of the women Ruth referred to as "false witnesses," whose testimony may have "infatuated" (misled) some members of the jury, it may be relevant to briefly relate the details of another tragedy that seems to have touched both the Clough and Challis families. Both families were original settlers in the Salisbury area, and we shall see how their common relationship to another family, the Dows, turned into a tragedy.

In 1755, Ruth's second cousin, Eliphaz Dow, was hanged for murdering Peter Clough of Hampton Falls. Two of Ruth's great-aunts, Mary and Hannah Challis, had successively married one Joseph Dow of that part of Hampton now known as South Seabrook.[110] The Dow family was a prominent Quaker family, as were some of the Challises. Probate records show land being sold and resold between Phillip Watson-Challis (Ruth's great-grandfather) and Joseph Dow. Both Mary and Hannah became Quakers when they married Joseph. This alone may have contributed to disputes between the Cloughs and the Dows and Challises—practicing Quakers were frequently persecuted.

Hannah Challis Dow appears in New Hampshire court records in 1700, at which time there was an order issued for her to appear before the Court of Quarter Sessions to answer to the charge of having committed fornication.[111] Unable to locate Hannah, who most probably had married Joseph Dow by then, she disappears from the provincial court records. Joseph and Hannah Challis Dow had six sons, one of them the notorious Eliphaz. Dow descendant Anna Adams, interested in preserving family history, left many of the records in a deserted family house in South Seabrook when she moved in with her son. While the house and records were destroyed by fire, she had copied one rhyme from an old schoolbook:

Elihu, Eliphaz, Amasa and Noah
Jesse, Zerviah, Bildad and Judah, too
These make up the Byfield crew[112]

In December 1754, Eliphaz was at his brother Noah's house when Peter Clough, a fisherman from Hampton Falls, came to the house in search of Eliphaz, whom he accused of killing one of his cows. There appears to have been a history both of Eliphaz' general character as disorderly and a ne'er-do-well and of an ongoing feud between Peter and Eliphaz.[113] When Clough challenged Eliphaz to settle the matter outside the house, all three men went outside, where an argument continued; the headstrong Eliphaz picked up Noah's hoe and struck Peter in the head, resulting in his death. Arrested, tried and convicted, Eliphaz Dow was hanged at the gallows on May 8, 1755, in the area of South and Middle Roads in Portsmouth and buried in the road. Work done on the road in the twentieth century uncovered the remains of a man thought to be Eliphaz. According to the *Boston Post* obituary, Eliphaz "died as he had lived, a stupid and hardened creature" who refused even to hear the execution sermon preached by Reverend Samuel Langdon, minister of the North Church. Newspaper reports claim that there were some ten thousand persons who witnessed this hanging.[114]

Thus we have the ingredients for jealousy and grudges between the birth families of Ruth Blay and Benjamin Clough. As families intermarried over the decades, grievances their members may have had with other families in the area often carried over. The Clough surname appears in many of the towns in which Ruth, her sisters and their husbands came to reside. In particular, Benjamin Clough, his wife Olive and sisters Sarah and Rachel came to play a significant role in the arrest and trial of Ruth Blay. Coincidence or old grievances being settled? It can probably never be established, but the case can be made that Benjamin and Olive had something to gain, if only the chance to raise their own social status in the small town of South Hampton, which had "warned them out" just three years prior to Ruth's trial. While the warning does not mention specifics, it does indicate that they were not legal inhabitants.[115]

By 1768, they seem to have finally settled there legally, and the barn in which Ruth gave birth is referred to in court records as the "barn of one Benjamin Clough." Olive's father was William Graves, who owned a considerable amount of property in South Hampton. We can conjecture that Benjamin might have purchased or been given some of Graves's property adjacent to the Reuben Currier home. At any rate, the Cloughs— Benjamin, Olive and Benjamin's sisters Sarah and Rachel—must have made a formidable group of witnesses. Some of these women may even have been students of Ruth's.

Untangling the genealogical web of witnesses' surnames is a frustrating and unfinished challenge. We can determine that the Clough, Currier, Merrill and Brown families intermarried, as did the French, Morrill, Chase and Currier families. It does seem that some family lines may have been drawn in Ruth's case. Although she was purportedly boarding with the Currier family, the French family must have sided with her or at least remained neutral, as it is with them that she left the blue quilt. No member of the French family was called to testify, although two of them, James and Moses, were present for the postmortem inquisition.

Ruth suggests that these "two women" were driven to falsely testify by "Prejudice, Jealousy or something else," and this might imply that Ruth and these women were of different social, economic or educational status. Ruth was clearly the better educated, and her position as a teacher, possibly even their teacher at one time, may have afforded the younger women some satisfaction. The "jealousy" charge is interesting, and had Ruth revealed the paternity of her infant, that accusation might be less cryptic. Was the father someone these young women had themselves fancied or been rejected by? Or was he someone, as I have previously suggested, whose status was higher even than Ruth's and far beyond the reach of these young rural women? Or were the emotions simply a reflection of old wounds between the families being reopened? Here the trail ends—with more questions than answers—but always with the hope that someone somewhere will read about Ruth's life and family and through family oral tradition or actual letters and diaries be able to pick up the thread and stitch in those empty spaces.

Epilogue

For many years, a blue quilted piece of fabric that purportedly had belonged to Ruth remained in the care of the French family's women. The last of these, Annie French, gave the remaining piece of quilt to local South Hampton historian Sadie Embree. Sadie, in turn, wisely chose to place the quilt in the hands of the Portsmouth Historical Society, where it has been carefully preserved since 1971. Torn in places—some pieces were cut off and given to others before its rescue—the quilt remnant is a piece of faded imported indigo blue wool backed by undyed wool. Such quilted petticoats were popular during the mid-1700s, sometimes worn alone for added warmth and sometimes as decorative wear under open-fronted skirts. Certainly, women could buy fabric already quilted, but quilt expert Lynne Bassett in her book *Northern Comfort* suggests that quilted petticoats may have been responsible for the first surge of home-based quilting.[116] It was a less expensive route to fashion, and Ruth, a sempstress, or her mother, a tailor, may have initially quilted the fabric.

While impossible to verify without a doubt that this belonged to Ruth Blay, it has been authenticated by textile expert Jane Nylander as a mid-eighteenth-century petticoat that was reseamed to serve as a coverlet,[117] and there is no reason not to believe its origin, as it was passed down through several generations of one family whose home was just across the road and up a short distance from the Currier/Clough structures. Again, Ruth stated in her

Annie French, of the family that cared for the quilt over the years, and young Frank Dennett holding what is believed to be Ruth Blay's quilt. *Courtesy of the South Hampton Library.*

declaration that she could have produced clothing made for her infant and the woman in whose keeping they were, and the French family not only were not called to testify, but it is also in their family that we find the quilt. It may have been part of a garment worn during the winter months of her pregnancy or perhaps an older petticoat that had been cut and restructured as a covering for her expected infant. It is not fancy work, but it is well done and must have originally been quite handsome. As far as is now known, this textile fragment is the only tangible evidence of the woman who endured this unfortunate fate.

The governor to whom Ruth expressed appreciation for the three reprieves granted, John Wentworth, went on to charter Dartmouth College, build a country estate in Wolfeboro, New Hampshire, and vastly improve the roads between Portsmouth and points north and west. However, the events leading up to the Revolution as well as administrative changes in England resulted in the Wentworth family losing favor with the king and thus losing the Royal Navy's mast contract, thereby quickly eroding Wentworth's control over subcontracts in frontier New Hampshire. Frustrated and frightened by his loss of power, as well as the growing anti-British sentiment, John Wentworth

Ruth's blue quilt. Whether the baby was found wrapped in it or whether it was a petticoat she had refashioned as a blanket for the baby is unknown, but it remained in the French family until it was given to Sadie Embree, South Hampton historian, who in turn gave it to the Portsmouth Historical Society. *Photograph by author. Courtesy of Portsmouth Historical Association.*

fled to England. He would later return to Nova Scotia, where he served as governor until his death in 1820.

The king's attorney, Wyseman Claggett, converted to the Patriot cause. He moved to Litchfield and was chosen a member of the last provincial assembly under British government and subsequently of the Third and Fifth Provincial Congresses. Following the Revolution, he helped the fledgling state establish its governing body, serving as attorney general and later as the elected representative to the House from Merrimack and Bedford. In 1781, he became the first and only solicitor general for the state. Claggett died in his Litchfield home in 1784.

Sheriff Thomas Packer died a wealthy man in 1771 and was buried in the Wentworth tomb at St. John's Episcopal Church in Portsmouth. His will, hotly contested by his son Thomas Packer Jr., left everything to the Wentworth family, to whom he felt indebted for his prominence and prosperity.

Reverend Page continued to minister to his parish in Hawke until 1782. In that year, a new epidemic, smallpox, spread throughout the province. Reverend Page contracted it while tending to the suffering of one of his parishioners and died within days. He is buried in Danville's old cemetery, up the road from the meetinghouse at which he preached.

Lydia Blay, Ruth's mother, may have moved to the Richford, Vermont area with her daughter Mary and grandson Stephen Blaisdell after Nathaniel Blaisdell's death in 1786. Although she would have been eighty-five years old, it would have been difficult for her to remain in this region in which she had witnessed so much pain. If she died before Mary made the move, I have yet to find a death record or burial site for her.

If Ruth's death served any purpose, it was to arouse public awareness of the inequity of a long-outdated law. The memory of Ruth and others who had suffered her fate echoed through the years and inspired a significant revision in New Hampshire's legal code. In the new law of 1791, the punishment for concealing a baby would be standing on the gallows with a rope around the neck for one hour and imprisonment not to exceed two years.[118]

In an analysis of Carol Berkin's book *First Generations: Women in Colonial America*, Yale professor emeritus Edmund S. Morgan states, "Bearing children is imposed on women by God or nature or biology, whether in Boston or Burma, but women's subjection to men, whether in the state or in the family, is imposed by ideas and attitudes that have no other basis than a society's acceptance of them."[119]

In the eighteenth century and also more recently, the death penalty has been applied most often to persons on the fringes of society—people marginalized by gender, race, social, economic or educational status or a combination thereof. Unfortunately, Ruth was a victim of her gender, her society and her time.

Ruth's Story as Retold Through Time

R uth's story captured the imagination of succeeding generations and has been transformed into several versions with much exaggeration and embellishment, but it is this oral tradition—the story as remembered and retold through time—that has served the worthy cause of keeping the story alive. Indeed, had I not been introduced to the story through a nineteenth-century account, I would have remained ignorant of the factual story. Apart from the account of the trial, sentencing, reprieves, confession and execution, the newspapers of her day seem to have dropped the story. It is given perfunctory mention by Samuel Lane in his journal for the year 1768: "Ruth Blay hanged."[120]

Annals of Portsmouth, by Nathaniel Adams, was published in 1825 and reports the following for the year 1768:

> *Friday, December 30th. Ruth Blay, of South Hampton, was executed in pursuance of the sentence of death, pronounced upon her by the Superior Court at August term last. She was indicted for concealing the birth of a bastard child, so that it might not come to light, whether the said child was born alive or not. Wiseman Claggett, Esquire, was the King's Attorney, who conducted the prosecution. The Court were, Theodore Atkinson, Chief Justice, Thomas Wallingford, Meshech Weare, and Leverett Hubbard,*

Justices. She was convicted by the verdict of a jury, and sentenced to be hanged by the neck until she should be dead. This sentence was executed by Sheriff Thomas Packer, Sheriff of the province, on a ridge of high land in a field, belonging to the south parish, lying on the south road, and on the road leading to Little-Harbour. She was buried in the same field, near the bottom of the hill. A vast concourse of people attended.[121]

This account is drawn chiefly from the provincial papers. It is the earliest of the published retellings and, although sparse, is probably the most accurate. It is here that we find the first mention of Ruth's burial spot at the bottom of the hill.

The *New Hampshire Sentinel* in January 1836 lists all of the public executions occurring in New Hampshire and is the first reference I have found that suggests that Ruth was prematurely hanged minutes before a pardon arrived from the governor. It reads as follows:

1768, December 30. Ruth Blay, of South Hampton, was executed for concealing the birth of a bastard child, so that it might not come to light whether the said child was born alive or dead. She was deprived of a pardon in consequence of the precipitancy of the Sheriff, Packer, who declared he would not lose his dinner, and swung her off 15 minutes before the time assigned. The pardon reached his hands in about ten minutes. She was hung on a high ridge of land in Portsmouth. A vast concourse of people attended.

No other one of the above executions produced a tenth part of the excitement, as was witnessed when Ruth Blay suffered death. All the circumstances in her case were calculated to enlist sympathy, although her crime was heinous. She was young, beautiful, interesting, and well educated; and from the hour of her arrest to the moment of her death, she wept almost constantly. The misfortune which led to her crime, was one where plighted faith had overreached confiding love; and the keen sufferings of a sensitive mind borne in solitude and tears from the moment of her first error, until the day which witnessed her last crime, were deemed severe punishment, for one whose first fault was more the crime of a faithless lover than her own. But to crown the whole, she was hung by a Sheriff, who, rather than dine later than usual, launched her into eternity fifteen minutes before the expiration of the time limiting her execution, and in five minutes after the fatal act a full pardon from the Governor reached the gallows upon which she was hanging.[122]

We are now sixty-eight years past the actual event, and the barebones story told by court records, provincial papers and period news accounts has begun to take on a life of its own, growing like a pearl from a grain of sand. She is "young" (she was thirty-one); she is "beautiful" (according to what source?); she is "interesting" (source?); "she wept almost constantly" (possibly!); she has "a sensitive mind" and a "faithless lover" (source? Certainly Ruth doesn't say this); and Sheriff Packer is now seen as a heartless, cruel "villain" who must perform the act quickly so as not to miss his dinner. For the first time, there is mention of a "pardon" arriving from the governor moments after she is hanged. This is a huge sticking point and makes for a tragic story, but there is no extant evidence in any of the court records or newspapers from that period to verify a pardon—or any of the other colorful but groundless details of this account.

In 1847, John Greenleaf Whittier published a book, *The Supernaturalism of New England*, in which he mentions yet another "Ruth Blaye" tale wherein the wraith of her dead infant appeared at the window while she was visiting with friends, causing her to confess to its murder:

There are those yet living in this very neighborhood who remember, and relate with an awe which half a century has not abated, the story of Ruth Blaye, the GHOST CHILD! Ruth was a young woman of lively temperament and some personal beauty. While engaged as the teacher in the little town of Southampton, N.H., (whose hills roughen the horizon with their snowy outline within view of my window at this very moment), she was invited to spend an evening at the dwelling of one of her associates. Suddenly, in the midst of unwonted gaiety, the young schoolmistress uttered a frightful shriek, and was seen gazing with a countenance of intense horror at the open window; and pointing with her rigid, outstretched arm at an object which drew at once the attention of her companions. Upon the sill of the window, those present saw, or thought they saw, a dead infant which vanished before they could find words to express their surprise. The wretched Ruth was the first to break the silence. "It is mine—MINE—MY CHILD!" she shrieked; "he has come for me!" She gradually became more tranquil, but no effort availed to draw from her the terrible secret which was evidently connected with the apparition. She was soon after arrested and brought to trial for the crime of child-murder, found guilty, and executed at Portsmouth, N.H.[123]

Obviously, this is oral tradition at work—and at its best! If one can extract any truth from it, it might be that Ruth was, in fact, teaching while she stayed in South Hampton, perhaps even doing so in the Clough barn, as there are other instances of barns being used as schoolrooms when the weather was temperate. If true in this case, that may explain how the story changed in some accounts to say that the baby was found hidden in Miss Blay's *classroom*.

The story of Ruth Blay continued to be embellished in 1859 when Charles Brewster published a compilation of his historical essays entitled *Rambles about Portsmouth Sketches of Persons, Localities, and Incidents of Two Centuries: Tradition and Unpublished Documents Principally from Portsmouth, N.H.* In this book, which despite its many inaccuracies remains an excellent reference, the story of Ruth Blay is told as most people have come to understand it. In a mixture of fact, fantasy and a creative blend of the two, Brewster relates Ruth's story as follows:

> *On that most elevated spot on the north side of the Cemetery* [South Cemetery], *just above the row of tombs, a gallows was once erected—and there, amid a thousand spectators, on the 30ᵗʰ of December, 1768, an unfortunate girl was hung—a poor, misguided girl of better conscience than many who have marble monuments with gilded inscriptions to perpetuate their memory.*
>
> *In August, 1768, Ruth Blay of South Hampton, was indicted for concealing the death of an illegitimate child, whereby it might not be known whether it were born alive or not. The English statute prescribed the penalty of death for this offence...The exordium of Attorney General Claggett in the above prosecution is still remembered for its pompous solemnity. "He called heaven to witness, that he was discharging a duty that he owed his country, his King, and his God."*
>
> *An old lady who was present at the execution of Ruth Blay, said—as Ruth was carried through the streets, her shrieks filled the air. She was dressed in silk, and was driven under the gallows in a cart. Public sympathy was awakened for her, and her friends had procured from the Governor a reprieve, which would have soon resulted in her pardon—for circumstances afterwards showed that her child was probably still-born, and she was*

not a murderer. The hour for her execution arrived, and the sheriff, not wishing, it is said, to be late to his dinner, ordered the cart to be driven away, and the unfortunate woman was left hanging from the gallows. If we are rightly informed, she was a girl of good education for her day, having been a school-mistress. The indignation of the populace can hardly be conceived when it was ascertained that a reprieve from the governor came a few minutes after her spirit had been hastened away. They gathered that evening around the residence of Sheriff Packer…and an effigy was there erected bearing this inscription:

Am I to lose my dinner
This woman for to hang?
Come draw away the cart, my boys—
Don't stop to say Amen.
Draw away, draw away the cart![124]

Also in that year, 1859, Albert Laighton, a Portsmouth poet, published his new volume of poems that included the following, introduced by an extract from *Brewster's Rambles* no. 59.

The Ballad of Ruth Blay

In the worn and dusty annals
Of our old and quiet town,
With its streets of leafy beauty,
And its houses quaint and brown,—

With its dear associations,
Hallowed by the touch of Time,—
You may read this thrilling legend,
This sad tale of wrong and crime.

In the drear month of December,
Ninety years ago to-day,
Hundreds of the village people
Saw the hanging of Ruth Blay;—

Saw her clothed in silk and satin,
Borne beneath the gallows-tree,
Dressed as in her wedding garments,
Soon the bride of Death to be;—the

Saw her tears of shame and anguish
Heard her shrieks of wild despair,
Echo thro' the neighboring woodlands,
Thrill the clear and frosty air.

Till their hearts were moved to pity
At her fear and agony:
"Doomed to die," they said, "unjustly,
Weak, but innocent is she."

When at last, in tones of warning,
From its high and airy tower,
Slowly, with its tongue of iron,
Tolled the bell the fatal hour;—

Like the sound of distant billows,
When the storm is wild and loud,
Breaking on the rocky headland,
Ran a murmur through the crowd.

And a voice among them shouted,
"Pause before the deed is done;
We have asked reprieve and pardon
For the poor misguided one."

But these words of Sheriff Packer
Rang above the swelling noise:
"Must I wait and lose my dinner?
Draw away the cart, my boys!"

Fold thy hands in prayer, O woman!
Take thy last look at the sea;

108

Take thy last look of the landscape
God be merciful to thee!

Stifled groans, a gasp, a shudder,
And the guilty deed was done;
On a scene of cruel murder
Coldly looked the winter sun.

Then the people, pale with horror,
Looked with sudden awe behind,
As a field of grain in Autumn
Turns before a passing wind;

For distinctly in the distance,
In the long and frozen street,
They could hear the ringing echoes
Of a horse's sounding feet.

Nearer came the sound and louder
Till a steed with panting breath,
From its sides the white foam dripping,
Halted at the scene of death;

And a messenger alighted,
Crying to the crowd, "Make way!
This I bear to Sheriff Packer;
'Tis a pardon for Ruth Blay!"

But they answered not nor heeded,
For the last fond hope had fled;
In their deep and speechless sorrow,
Pointing only to the dead.

And that night with burning bosoms,
Muttering curses fierce and loud,
At the house of Sheriff Packer
Gathered the Indignant crowd,—

Shouting, as upon a gallows
A grim effigy they bore,
"Be the name of Thomas Packer
A reproach forevermore!"[125]

This poem was reprinted in the *Portsmouth Journal of Literature and Politics* and came to be regarded as the definitive version of the story; the truth of it was not questioned—poetic license ruled.

With this ballad, which captured Brewster's account in rhyme, Ruth's now ninety-year-old story reached new dramatic heights. In addition to the questionable "pardon" arriving too late because of a sheriff impatient for his dinner, we have a mob scene in front the man's home at the corner of Pleasant and Court Streets, bearing an effigy of the sheriff. If there is any truth to this, the evidence is buried in time. Certainly the newspapers were not reporting it. To put to rest the story that Sheriff Packer hurried the hanging for whatever reason, we have only to read the final reprieve issued by Governor Wentworth. It clearly reads that the execution was to be carried out between the hours of ten and two o'clock, even though the original sentence specified between twelve and two o'clock. Indeed the "12" is crossed out and "10" inserted in Packer's report of the execution, but he clearly did this to accurately reflect the final order from the governor, not to justify an early execution.

The year 1859 appears to have been a banner year for Ruth Blay retrospectives. In the *Portsmouth Journal of Literature and Politics* for May 7, 1859, we find the suggestion that Brewster's *Rambles About Portsmouth* contains a number of stories that a novelist could expand upon, one of them being that of Ruth Blay. It continues to say that this has indeed resulted in a novel by Dr. Frank Fuller, which will run "between three and four hundred pages."[126] What happened to this manuscript is, unfortunately, unknown. Quite possibly it was never published, although it would be of interest to know exactly how he might have addressed the various questions open to speculation.

In 1883, Portsmouth author Thomas Bailey Aldrich published *An Old Town by the Sea*, in which he repeats the Brewster/Laighton version of the story, adding only that the effigy "was afterward paraded through the streets."[127]

In 1926, Ralph May published *Early Portsmouth History*, and the story of Ruth Blay is reduced, rather than expanded, to the following: "In 1768 Ruth Blay, of tragic story and famed in versed, is said to have been executed."

RUTH'S STORY AS RETOLD THROUGH TIME

Thus, 158 years after the event, Ruth is rather summarily dismissed and doubt cast as to whether the execution had, in fact, even taken place![128]

Alton Blackington, author of *Yankee Yarns*, published in 1954, included the Ruth Blay story and spun an inaccurate, highly embellished account complete with "quotes" from some of the original players! It perpetuates the old inaccuracies and creates a few more but makes for a "good read."[129]

Finally, South Hampton historian Sadie Embree made a worthy attempt to establish the facts in a 1971 paper entitled "The Ruth Blay Story," which can be found at the South Hampton Library. The typewritten transcripts of many of the court records are here recorded, with commentary. Although there are some inaccuracies, it is the first attempt to set the record straight by going to the source at the state archives.[130]

Despite nineteenth-century renditions to the contrary, there is no mention of a fourth reprieve or pardon anywhere in the official record of her case found in the New Hampshire State Archives. Sheriff Packer's January 3 report of the execution mentions only his original order and the three reprieves.[131] If any document arrived after the hanging, it is just as likely to have been an order to proceed with the execution. However, it is easy to see how the aroused crowd might have misinterpreted it as a pardon.

In more recent times, a play and a screenplay have been written about Ruth's story, and of course, she is remembered in the walkabout tours of Portsmouth's ghostly haunts. While there is a blend of fact and fiction in all of these, the true story of Ruth Blay is dramatic and poignant enough to stand on its own. One may wish for more clarity and feel frustrated by questions that beg for answers, but it is up to each reader of her story to supply these as his or her imagination sees fit.

In the words of Amartya Sen in his book *The Idea of Justice*:

Resistance to injustice typically draws on both indignation and argument. Frustration and ire can help to motivate us, and yet ultimately we have to rely, for both assessment and effectiveness, on reasoned scrutiny to obtain a plausible and sustainable understanding of the basis of those complaints… and what can be done to address the underlying problem.[132]

Initially, my search was fueled by indignant outrage. Years of research later, that outrage has become tempered by a better understanding of the historical culture and climate in which Ruth lived and died. Certainly what happened to her was not "just" on many levels. Indeed, she was the victim of a biased justice system. The story as repeated through time rewrote history, no doubt with good intentions, to depict clear villains and victims, something that often happens when viewing historical events in retrospect. However, without this oral and written tradition of storytelling, Ruth, like so many other similar women, would have been lost to time. So I am indebted to both the folkloric tradition and to the preservation of archival records that allowed me to separate fact from fiction. The truth, as always, lies somewhere in between.

Notes

Introduction

1. Bolton and Coe, *American Samplers*, 279.
2. Bouton, *Provincial Papers*, 1764–1776.
3. Brewster and Hackett, *Rambles About Portsmouth*, 287–88.
4. Ibid.
5. Adams and Hodgdon, *Annals of Portsmouth*, 224.
6. *New Hampshire Gazette*, December 23, 1768.
7. Benes, with Dublin Seminar, *Life on the Streets and Commons*, 97.
8. *Boston Post Boy*, January 2, 1769.

Chapter 1

9. Bolton and Coe, *American Samplers*, 346.
10. Coffin and Bartlett, *A Sketch of the History of Newbury*, 197–222.
11. Chase and Chamberlain, comps., *Seven Generations*, 41.
12. Ibid.
13. Probate Records, Essex County, Massachusetts, docket no. 5132.
14. *Vital Records of Haverill*, vol. 1, 35.

CHAPTER 2

15. Bolton and Coe, *American Samplers*, 298.
16. Coffin and Bartlett, *A Sketch of the History of Newbury*, 204.
17. *New England Weekly Journal*, March 28, 1738.
18. Chase, *History of Haverhill*, 279.
19. *Essex Antiquarian* 1, "Throat Distemper in Haverill," 10.
20. Coffin and Bartlett, *A Sketch of the History of Newbury*, 208.

CHAPTER 3

21. Bolton and Coe, *American Samplers*, 278.
22. Coffin and Bartlett, *A Sketch of the History of Newbury*, 209.
23. Rutman, ed., *The Great Awakening*, 45.
24. Goen, *Revivalism and Separatism in New England*, 19–26.
25. Coffin and Bartlett, *A Sketch of the History of Newbury*, 212.
26. Ibid.
27. Shipton, *New England Life*, 126.
28. Goen, *Revivalism and Separatism in New England*, 101.
29. Ibid., 63.
30. Brainerd and Edwards, *Life and Diary of David Brainerd*, 49–50.
31. Seeman, *Pious Persuasions*, 158.
32. Gillies, *Memoirs of Reverend George Whitefield*, 219.
33. Coffin and Bartlett, *A Sketch of the History of Newbury*, 238.
34. Renfro, *Life and Works of Phillis Wheatley*, 50.
35. Sloan, *Great Awakening*, 1.
36. Seeman, *Pious Persuasions*, 175.
37. Ibid., 177.

CHAPTER 4

38. Bolton and Coe, *American Samplers*, 260.
39. Probate Records, Essex County, Mass., docket no. 2643.
40. Ulrich, *Good Wives*, 9–10.

41. Sprigg, *Domestick Beings*, 43. For a sampling from the diaries of three eighteenth-century women and illustrations of common household furnishings, see *Domestick Beings* in its entirety.
42. Ibid., 43.
43. Ibid., 36.
44. Warnings, South Hampton, 1744, New Hampshire Division of Archives and Records Management, Concord, New Hampshire (hereafter cited as State Archives).
45. *Vital Records of the Town of South Hampton*, 52.
46. *Vital Records of Newbury, Massachusetts*, vol. 2, 549.
47. *Vital Records of the Town of South Hampton*, 52.
48. *Essex Antiquarian* 10, "Notes," 137.
49. Metcalfe, *Probate Records*, vol. 2, 305.
50. Bell, *Facts Relating to the Early History of Chester*, 26.

CHAPTER 5

51. "Acts and Laws of His Majesty's Province," 120.
52. Bolton and Coe, *American Samplers*, 267.
53. Chase, *History of Chester*, 277.
54. "Acts and Laws of His Majesty's Province."
55. Monaghan, *Learning to Read and Write*, 13, 81–111.
56. Ibid., 192.
57. Bell, *Facts Relating to the Early History of Chester*, 26.
58. Holmes, *A View from Meeting House Hill*, 269.
59. *Early Town Records of Danville*, microfilm, 709.

CHAPTER 6

60. Bolton and Coe, *American Samplers*, 298.
61. Ulrich and Stabler, "'Girling of It,'" 25.
62. Rich, *History of Danville*, 16.
63. Shipton, *New England Life*, vol. 15, *1761–1763*, 87–88.
64. Rich, *History of Danville*, 16.
65. Ulrich, *Good Wives*, 89–92.

CHAPTER 7

66. Bolton and Coe, *American Samplers*, 297.
67. Currier, *Currier Family Records*, vol. 1, 278; 284.
68. Ibid., 247.
69. Ulrich, *Good Wives*, 127.
70. Dearborn, *History of Salisbury*, 691–92.
71. "Inquisition on the Body of a Child supposed of Ruth Blay," June 14, 1768 (hereafter cited as Blay Case), State Archives.
72. Petitions for reimbursement, from William Cooper and others, are summarized in "Journal of the House" in Provincial State Papers, vol. 7, 206. The individual manuscript petitions are on file at the State Archives.
73. Petition requesting reimbursement, Josiah Bartlett, March 11, 1769. State Archives.
74. Petition requesting reimbursement, Benjamin Clough, March 10, 1769. All petitions were granted with the exception of Samuel Hall's, mentioned in the first chapter. State Archives.

CHAPTER 8

75. Bolton and Coe, *American Samplers*, 335.
76. Rogers, *Glimpses of an Old Social Capital*, 46.
77. *Samuel Lane, Almanack, December, 1768.*

CHAPTER 9

78. Bolton and Coe, *American Samplers*, 328.
79. Adams and Hodgdon, *Annals of Portsmouth*, 172.
80. Early American Imprints. First Series. No. 4599. *"The Faith and Prayer of a Dying Malefactor: A sermon preach'd December 27, 1739. On occasion of the execution of two criminals, namely Sarah Simpson and Penelope Kenny, and in the hearing of the former. By William Shurtleff, A.M. Pastor of a church in Portsmouth, New-Hampshire; To which is annex'd a brief narrative concerning the said criminals: and a preface by the Reverend Mr. Fitch* (Boston, MA: J. Draper, 1740).
81. Ibid.

82. Ibid.
83. Ibid.
84. *The Faith and Prayer of a Dying Malefactor.*
85. *Boston Post Boy*, August 20, 1739.
86. "Acts and Laws of His Majesty's Province," 15.
87. Hoffer and Hull, *Murdering Mothers*, 77–79.
88. "Acts and Laws of His Majesty's Province," 12.
89. Hoffer and Hull, *Murdering Mothers*, 68–74.
90. Ibid. 63.
91. State Archives, Records of the Superior Court of Judicature, 1764–1767, file no. 11994.
92. Ibid.
93. State Archives, Records of the Superior Court of Judicature, 1763–1767, file no. 026336.
94. State Archives, Records of the Superior Court of Judicature, 1763–1767, vol. F, 110–11.

CHAPTER 10

95. Bolton and Coe, *American Samplers*, 319.
96. Adams and Hodgdon, *Annals of Portsmouth*, 199.
97. State Archives, Records of the Superior Court of Judicature, vol. F, 203.
98. Ibid.
99. Bell, *Bench and Bar of New Hampshire*, 266.
100. *New Hampshire Gazette*, September 23, 1768.
101. Ibid.
102. State Archives, Minutes, Superior Court, August 1768; Blay Case.
103. State Archives, Superior Court of Judicature, vol., F, 203–4.
104. Ibid., "Warrant (writ) of execution from the court to the sheriff, September 3, 1768," Blay Case. Note that the date on this document is in error and was most certainly intended to read September 23.

Chapter 11

105. Bolton and Coe, *American Samplers*, 264.
106. This reprieve and two others are in the Blay case file at the State Archives. All three set the time of execution between 10:00 a.m. and 2:00 p.m.
107. Ibid.
108. *The Declaration and Confession of Ruth Blay*, a broadside, was printed by Daniel Fowle in Portsmouth, New Hampshire, at 2:00 a.m. on December 30, 1768. An original of this broadside is located at the Phillips Library, Peabody-Essex Museum, Salem, Massachusetts. This one probably appeared in the *Essex Gazette*. Another version is located in the Harry Houdini Collection, University of Texas.

Chapter 12

109. Bolton and Coe, *American Samplers*, 330.
110. Sanborn, "Joseph Dow's Second Wife," 98–104.
111. Ibid., 100.
112. Ibid., 104.
113. Ibid., 105.
114. Ibid., 106. Taken from *Index of Obituaries*, vol. 2, 318.
115. Warnings, South Hampton, March 1765, State Archives.

Epilogue

116. Bassett, *Northern Comfort*, 15.
117. The author wishes to thank textile expert Jane Nylander for identifying the type and age of the remnant.
118. Metcalf, *Laws of New Hampshire*, vol. 5, *First Constitutional Period*, 596–97.
119. Morgan, *Genuine Article*, 42.

RUTH'S STORY AS RETOLD THROUGH TIME

120. *Samuel Lane, Almanack, December, 1768.*
121. Adams and Hodgdon, *Annals of Portsmouth*, 224.
122. *New Hampshire Sentinel*, January 21, 1836, 2.
123. Whittier, *Supernaturalism of New England*, 40–41.
124. Brewster and Hackett, *Rambles About Portsmouth*, 287–92.
125. Laighton, "Ruth Blay," *Journal of Literature and Politics*, April 23, 1859, 1, column 6.
126. Brewster, *Journal of Literature and Politics*, 1892, 2; column 2.
127. Aldrich, *Old Town by the Sea*, 74.
128. May, *Early Portsmouth History*, 238.
129. Blackington, *Yankee Yarns*, 193–201.
130. Embree, *Ruth Blay Story.*
131. Thomas Packer's return (report) appears at the end of the original warrant, January 3, 1769, State Archives; Blay Case.
132. Sen, *Idea of Justice*, 390.

Bibliography

"Acts and Laws of His Majesty's Province of New Hampshire in New England." Portsmouth, NH: Daniel Fowle, 1761.

Adams, Nathaniel, and George E. Hodgdon. *Annals of Portsmouth: A History of Portsmouth*. Portsmouth, NH: Portsmouth Journal, 1886.

Aldrich, Thomas Bailey. *An Old Town by the Sea*. Boston, MA: Houghton, Mifflin, and Company, 1894.

Bailyn, Bernard. *The ideological Origins of the American Revolution*. Cambridge, MA: Belknap Press of Harvard University Press, 1967.

Bassett, Lynne Z., Jack Larkin and Thomas Neill. *Northern Comfort: New England's Early Quilts, 1780–1850*. From the Collection of Old Sturbridge Village. Nashville, TN: Rutledge Hill Press, 1998.

Bell, Charles H. *The Bench and Bar of New Hampshire*. Boston, MA: Houghton, Mifflin, and Company, 1894.

———. *Facts Relating to the Early History of Chester, N.H.* Concord, NH: G. Parker Lyon for the New Hampshire Historical Society, 1863.

Benes, Peter, ed. "Families and Children." Dublin Seminar for New England Folklife, Annual Proceedings. Boston, MA: Boston University, 1988.

———. "Life on the Streets and Commons, 1600 to the Present." Dublin Seminar for New England Folklife, Annual Proceedings. Boston, MA: Boston University, 2007.

Blackington, Alton H. *Yankee Yarns.* New York: Dodd, Mead, 1954.

Bolton, Ethel Stanwood, and Eva Johnston Coe. *American Samplers.* Boston, MA: Society of the Colonial Dames of America, 1921.

Bouton, Nathaniel, ed. *Provincial Papers, Documents and Records Relating to the Province of New Hampshire from 1764 to 1776.* Vol. 7. Nashua, NH: Owen C. Moore, State Printer, 1873.

Brainerd, David, and Jonathan Edwards. *The Life and Diary of David Brainerd.* Chicago, IL: Moody Press, 1949.

Brewster, Charles W., and William H.Y. Hackett. *Rambles About Portsmouth. Sketches of Persons, Localities and Incidents of Two Centuries, Principally from Tradition and Unpublished Documents.* Second series. Bowie, MD: Heritage Books, 2000.

Chase, George Wingate. *The History of Haverhill, Massachusetts from Its First Settlement in 1640 to the Year 1860.* Haverhill, MA: self-published, 1861.

Chase, John Carroll. *History of Chester, New Hampshire including Auburn: Supplement to the History of Old Chester published 1869.* Derry, NH: self-published, 1926.

Chase, John Carroll, and George Walter Chamberlain, comps. *Seven Generations of the Descendants of Aquila and Thomas Chase.* Derry, NH: Record Publishing Company, 1928.

Coffin, Joshua, and Joseph Bartlett. *A Sketch of the History of Newbury, Newburyport, and West Newbury, from 1635 to 1845.* Boston, MA: S.G. Drake, 1845.

Currier, Philip Joseph. *Currier Family Records of U.S.A. and Canada.* Henniker, NH: P.J. Currier, 1984.

Dearborn, John J. *The History of Salisbury, New Hampshire from Date of Settlement to the Present Time.* Manchester, NH: William E. Moore, 1890.

Earle, Alice Morse. *Customs and Fashions in Old New England.* New York: Charles Scibner's Sons, 1893.

Early Town Records of Danville, N.H., 1760–1848. On microfilm at the New Hampshire State Library.

Embree, Sadie. "The Ruth Blay Story." Typewritten transcripts of court records with an introduction. South Hampton, NH: Friends of the Library, 1971.

Essex Antiquarian 1 (January 1897). "Throat Distemper in Haverill, 1735–1737," 10.

Essex Antiquarian 10 (July 1906). "Notes," 137.

Gillies, John. *Memoirs of the Life of the Reverend George Whitefield.* Middletown, CT: Hunt & Company, 1841.

Goen, C.C. *Revivalism and Separatism in New England, 1740–1800: Strict Congregationalist and Separate Baptists in the Great Awakening.* Yale Publications in Religion. New Haven, CT: Yale University, 1962.

Hoffer, Peter Charles, and N.E.H. Hull. *Murdering Mothers: Infanticide in England and New England, 1558–1803.* New York University School of Law Series in Legal History. New York: New York University Press, 1981.

Holmes, Richard. *A View from Meeting House Hill: A History of Sandown, New Hampshire.* Portsmouth, NH: Peter E. Randall, 1988.

Index of Obituaries in Boston newspapers, 1704–1795. 3 vols. Boston, MA: Boston Athenaeum, 1968.

May, Ralph. *Early Portsmouth History.* Boston, MA: C.E. Goodspeed & Company, 1926.

Metcalf, Henry, ed. *Laws of New Hampshire.* Vol. 5. *First Constitutional Period, 1784–1792.* Concord, NH: Rumford Press, 1916.

———. *Probate Records of the Province of New Hampshire.* Vol. 2. *1718–1740.* Bristol, NH: R.W. Musgrove, 1924.

Monaghan, E. Jennifer. *Learning to Read and Write in Colonial America. Studies in Print Culture and the History of the Book.* Amherst: University of Massachusetts Press, 2005.

Morgan, Edmund S. *The Genuine Article: A Historian Looks at Early America.* New York: W.W. Norton and Company, 2004.

New Hampshire Division of Archives and Records Management. "Inquisition on the Body of a Child supposed of Ruth Blay," June 14, 1768. Provincial Court Records, docket no. 4262. Concord, New Hampshire.

———. Warnings, South Hampton, 1744. Concord, New Hampshire.

Renfro, G. Herbert. *Life and Works of Phillis Wheatley.* Salem, NH: Ayer Company Publishers, Inc., n.d.

Rich, Ruth. *The History of Danville, N.H., on the Occasion of Its 215th Birthday (Hawke 1760–Danville 1975).* Rev. ed. Brookings, OR: R.J. Rich, 1999.

Rogers, Mary Cochrane. *Glimpses of an Old Social Capital (Portsmouth, New Hampshire) as Illustrated by the Life of the Reverend Arthur Browne and His Circle.* Boston, MA: printed for the subscribers, 1923.

Rutman, Darrett Bruce, ed. *The Great Awakening: Event and Exegesis.* New York: Wiley, 1970.

Samuel Lane's Almanack, December 1768. Typescript from original in Samuel Lane Papers, New Hampshire Historical Society. Concord, New Hampshire.

Sanborn, George, Jr. "Joseph Dow's Second Wife, and the Byfield Crew." *New Hampshire Genealogical Record* 7, no. 3 (1990): 98–104.

Seeman, Erik R. *Pious Persuasions: Laity and Clergy in Eighteenth-Century New England (Early America: History, Context, Culture)*. Baltimore, MD: Johns Hopkins University Press, 1999.

Sen, Amartya. *The Idea of Justice*. Cambridge, MA: Belknap Press of Harvard University Press, 2009.

Shipton, Clifford. *New England Life in the 18th Century: Representative Biographies from Sibley's Harvard Graduates*. Cambridge, MA: Belknap Press of Harvard University Press, 1963.

Sloan, Douglas. *The Great Awakening and American Education: A Documentary History*. New York: Teachers College Press, Columbia University, 1973.

Sprigg, June. *Domestick Beings*. New York: Knopf, 1984.

Ulrich, Laurel. *Good Wives: Image and Reality in the Lives of Women in Northern New England, 1650–1750*. New York: Knopf, 1982.

Ulrich, Laurel Thatcher, and Lois Stabler. "'Girling of It' in Eighteenth-Century New England." Dublin Seminar for New England Folklife, Annual Proceedings, 1985. Boston, MA: Boston University, 1987.

Vital Records of Haverill, Massachusetts to the End of 1849. 2 vols. Topsfield, MA: Topsfield Historical Society, 1910.

Vital Records of Newbury, Massachusetts, to the End of the Year 1849. 2 vols. Salem, MA: Essex Institute, 1911.

Vital Records of the Town of South Hampton, 1743–1900. South Hampton, NH: Historical Committee of the South Hampton Friends of the Library, 1970.

Whittier, John Greenleaf. *The Supernaturalism of New England*. Edited and with an introduction by Edward Wagenknecht. Norman: University of Oklahoma Press, 1969.

ABOUT THE AUTHOR

C arolyn Marvin currently works as a research librarian at the Portsmouth Athenaeum in Portsmouth, New Hampshire, where she first came upon the story of Ruth Blay. Previously, she worked in both public and school libraries. Ms. Marvin lives in a tiny ivy-covered brick house in the Atlantic Heights Historic District of Portsmouth with her granddaughter Makenzie, three cats, Dante the Westie, three hamsters and two fish.

Visit us at
www.historypress.net

www.ingramcontent.com/pod-product-compliance
Lightning Source LLC
Chambersburg PA
CBHW060809100426
42813CB00004B/1003